John Hutton:

With every blessing
and good wish
on the occasion
of your Ordination
to the Priesthood.
Dec. 17. 1978.
Philip [illegible]

# Transport of Delight

Norwich Bus Stn
513
KNG 471D

JACK BURTON

# Transport of Delight

*SCM PRESS LTD*

334 01682 7
First published 1976
by SCM Press Ltd
58 Bloomsbury Street, London

Typeset by Gloucester Typesetting Company
and printed in Great Britain by
Fletcher & Son Ltd, Norwich

*TO JOYCE*
*my mother*

*Nothing would cause me more distress than to feel cut off from the vast mass of unbelievers.*

*Simone Weil*

# *INTRODUCTION*

This is a simple book about God, the church, and the world. It was written with two objects in mind. I have tried to illustrate the unity of existence – the glorious catholicity of human life in which work, sex, religion, humour, nature, sport, poetry, architecture, music, history, love and friendship form part of one brilliant whole, and are not isolated fragments of awareness. Here, therefore, are railway engines and high mass; here Christ is preached, and here is the cry of the redshank over the marshes; here is literature and good ale.

Secondly, I have attempted to outline my daily routine as a 'worker-priest', hoping that some may understand better why it is I have found greater fulfilment in my present unorthodox role (combining the sacred ministry with bus driving), than in the traditional pattern of ministry which I abandoned. This is a personal and revealing portrait, yet for that very reason I hope it may mirror some of the influences which – in the mid-seventies – are determining the form the church will assume in the future.

This diary is ninety-five per cent genuine. The journal method of presentation has not been employed purely as a literary device, and in only a few instances have I included earlier material which seemed relevant. Although the book says nothing about the terrifying problems (like world poverty and nuclear armaments) which confront mankind, I hope it is not trivial.

Unfortunately – though for obvious reasons – the best pieces have had to be omitted! The most intimate confidences, the most outrageous jokes, the funniest incidents, and the most precious expressions of affection are not included. But here is celebrated the turning of a year, day by day, with noteworthy events piercing periods of routine; and all is set against the cosmic background provided by the changing seasons and the psalms of evensong.

Modern Christians are divided at a deeper level than the old denominational differences. On the one hand are those who set the church over against the world as guardian and witness of a truth that is radically at odds with the perceptions prevalent elsewhere; who believe 'that it is in service not to the advancement of the human condition but to the kingdom of God, which is not of this world; that the institutions of the church are a bulwark against falsity, and its buildings a form of praise; that its integrity is ever endangered by uncritical assimilation of the "spirit of the age"; that its ancient rites and forms of worship should stand as both proclamation and guarantee that it will not defect'.[1]

On the other hand are those who believe the church, 'the community of the faithful, is a leaven in the world, properly active in all human concerns, a force to alleviate want and oppression as well as a light to illuminate men's minds; that its institutions are contingent and perhaps dispensable, its buildings plant to be judged by their utility; that it cannot be true to its mission if it fails to make sympathetic contact with the 'spirit of the age'; that its forms of worship must therefore undergo revision in conformity with contemporary styles'.[2] I am not naive enough to believe that my diary achieves any kind of satisfying synthesis of these positions; yet I would like to feel that both historic views find points of reference and a degree of faithful expression in the pages which follow.

*Colegate, Norwich*
*St Giles' Day, 1975*

Jack Robert Burton

PS I would like to express my thanks to John Bowden, Margaret Lydamore, Mark Hammer and Keith Parr of SCM Press for their enthusiasm, encouragement and advice; to Kevin Bird and all who have given photographic assistance; and to Molly, my wife, and Tony Lovett, my conductor, for putting up with me.

[1] *The Times*, 29 March 1975.
[2] Ibid.

*Monday 2 September 1974*

There's no reason why a journal *has* to begin on January 1st. I write when I get a flash of inspiration, and my inspiration came on September 2nd. So I have begun. I feel, in all fairness, that I ought to make perfectly clear at the outset the kind of person with whom you are dealing. This may prevent you paying for the book and wading patiently through many wearisome pages, only to be suddenly hurt and offended. I have to admit this evening – with no particular guilt or emotion, but with a certain surprise and mild amusement – that I am the kind of person who can be persuaded at the last moment to spend an evening in the pub rather than attend an ecclesiastical gathering. I didn't realize it myself until tonight. Anyhow, I have told you now: and it is as well that you should know, because these pages are certain to get worse instead of better.

I may have set a new record. Only one paragraph has been completed, and already I have slashed the viewing figures. To those who remain, let me introduce myself by saying simply that I am thirty-four, married, an ordained Methodist minister, and a full-time bus driver. After a tremendous battle, I was given reluctant permission by the church, six years ago, to serve in this dual capacity. I wanted to break out from the confines of the traditional ecclesiastical routine, and live close to people who didn't go to church. All other considerations apart, there was an immense personal risk involved. Because it was a genuine experiment, involving total economic dependence upon the world (and the freezing of my ministerial pension scheme!), it meant I was to be exposed to influences and situations that might overwhelm me. I have not escaped unscathed.

In the pages which follow, you will be able to gauge for yourself what six years of bus driving have done to me. I don't submit any more formal reports to the church. Nobody took much notice of them, and they were never mentioned. This was because I have achieved no results. To my immense disappointment, I have not persuaded one person regularly to attend divine service. But I have discovered what I long suspected – that it doesn't matter very much. I don't feel that my six years are totally lacking in achievement; my problem is how to represent the quality of a wide range of relationships in the form of statistics. Were this possible, I would be home and dry. As it is, I have nothing to show; and soon the pressure will be upon me again (it has never been far away) to return to the traditional work. All I can do is to invite you to live with me for a year. But if sex, and sin, and ribaldry, and coarseness disturb you, don't bother to stay. You'd do better to join those who left a little while ago on the first boat.

It was a thoroughly enjoyable couple of hours – one of the best evenings I've had this year. The church meeting was at 7.30; I was not due to take part, but ought to have been present. I left off work at 6.45, which in all honesty gave me little enough time to get home, wash, change, miss tea, and get out again; but such was my intention. Then in the bus station yard I met Steve and Charles, who offered to get me something for my cold. Steve had offered me a pint at the end of a shift some weeks before; I recalled that I had declined and hurried away to a meeting. This time I hesitated. Clergy are always hurrying to meetings. I yielded. Just a quick one. What an old story!

With empty stomachs we mellowed swiftly. We turned over our excuses one by one . . . a breakdown . . . some overtime . . . We discussed everything from barmaids to (of all things) aardvarks. I thought of the meeting, and was glad I was not there; if I never went to another I'd have attended my share. I glanced at my two companions. This, too, was meeting; closer meeting, probably, than anything happening at *the* meeting. I remember saying that all who hankered after promotion, or status, or an ever-increasing income were chasing things which ultimately didn't matter (like most meetings). 'But *this* matters,' I declared, with a sweep of the arm that took in bar, companions, friendship, laughter, relaxation, barriers down just a little, real meeting. They agreed.

*Tuesday 3 September*

I leapt aboard a passing bus on my way home at half past five this evening, and the conductor complained that he was ten minutes late. I stepped off the platform at the next stop while a long queue of people boarded the bus. The bell did not ring immediately, so – assuming the conductor to be busily collecting fares – I helped him and rang the bus away. After we had travelled some distance, it suddenly dawned on me that the conductor wasn't on the bus. He, too, had stepped off at the last stop – to inform an inspector that he was late! With a full standing load, and the city full of rush-hour traffic, the only sensible action was to stay with the bus and act as conductor for the remainder of that journey! The passengers were highly amused and full of witty remarks – while I shall never hear the end of it when the story gets round the garage. Apparently, after listening to the conductor, the inspector had asked: '*What* service did you say you are on?' '555,' he replied. The inspector was bewildered, and pointed to a bus disappearing in the distance: 'Not that 555 now going up there . . .?' Then it was the conductor's turn to be surprised.

*Wednesday 4 September*

I saw a good quotation on a poster at the university bus terminus this morning: 'True godliness does not turn men out of the world but enables them to live better in it and excites their endeavours to mend it' (William Penn, 1644–1718).

Sometimes, I feel I must be going serenely (though swiftly) mad. After a dull, cold day, the setting sun suddenly broke through the evening gloom. It fired a narrow strip of the western sky, and I was overjoyed, thinking I would be able to watch it sink towards the horizon. But a bank of heavy cloud appeared, and after only a few precious minutes the sun began to slip behind it. The effect was remarkably pronounced. It was like an oil lamp being turned down in a large room. The light of the world was being dimmed and extinguished. It seemed cruel and unbearable – a loss which would impoverish me for ever. And I could do nothing to prevent it. This day had gone, for all eternity.

Walking home late tonight I passed the old church of St Simon and St Jude which – together with the lime trees in the churchyard – was illuminated. Although I had seen it many times before, the scene was enchanting. The brilliant green of the floodlit leaves provided an exquisite setting for the shining, blue/black flint-stones. I wanted to cry.

*Thursday 5 September*

I looked in the church of St George, Tombland, this morning. I had never been inside before, and was thrilled beyond words. It was unashamedly Anglo-Catholic, with many side-altars, images, and banners, and the air was scented with incense; but it was not loud or vulgar, but homely. Unlike many modern places of worship it *felt* like a church; and my thoughts were lost in worship. 'Surely the Lord is in this place; and I knew it not.'

I visited an old man who is virtually house-bound. He told me: 'I asked the doctor if it was all right for me to have a Guinness every day. He said, "You can have two, so long as you pay for them." '

Again, the sun broke through late this evening. Although I was not moved so profoundly as last night, the sunset was more beautiful.

I made a slightly sarcastic remark to a young driver. He exclaimed: 'Bollicks – or testicles to you.' (He corrected himself hastily in deference to my calling.)

To be both intensely sensual and deeply spiritual is the secret of powerful personality. This potent blend does not produce hypocrisy, but integration and harmony, awareness and sensitivity.

Charles has had an unfortunate run of accidents, including one spectacular affair in which his bus finished up in a front garden facing the opposite direction, and another which involved the introduction of a large dent into the back of a police car. The conductor with whom I was working tonight told me of an occasion when he was with Charles (whose exploits are – to us – a source of gaiety). Their bus loudly clipped a van while negotiating a corner. The van, however, did not stop, and there wasn't a mark on the bus, so all was well. 'Aha,' I exclaimed, 'so he's had one or two we've not heard about?' 'Oh, yes,' replied the conductor, 'but he couldn't claim that as a hit. He didn't see it plunge to the ground and burst into flames. He could only claim that one as a probable!'

*Friday 6 September*

Is God male or female? The answer must be either 'both' or 'neither'. Jesus taught us to say 'Our Father', but we all realize that the limitations of human vocabulary are immense, and nobody supposes we can capture and define the 'nature' of the eternal reality we call 'God' in a few simple words – or even in many complicated ones! God is the ultimate, the indescribable. At best, our words are only signposts.

The writers of the book of Genesis declare that 'God created man in his own image . . . male and female created he them.' This interesting text doesn't mean that God has two legs, two arms, and a head; I think it *may* mean that men and women have the potentiality for displaying in their own lives – if ever so faintly – a reflection of the divine essence. He has made us capable of loving. But some people, reading that text, have proceeded to the assumption that God has made human beings in two halves, and that one person alone can never be more than an incomplete being, or a partial image of God, lacking fullness without a partner of the opposite sex. Much marriage doctrine has leant heavily in that direction. I reject utterly any such viewpoint. It has always struck me as unrealistic, impertinent nonsense. What seems much more obvious is that God has endowed each human person with a mixture of the traditional male and female characteristics. The balance of the mixture varies. It appears to follow fairly well-defined lines, but a mixture it is, in the one individual: and I am glad that it is so.

Among the traditional 'female characteristics' are traits like gentleness, tenderness, and compassion; among the traditional 'male characteristics' are the qualities of assertiveness and leadership. But imagine how unbearable a totally-male male would be – without a sweetening of patience and warmth! The only thing I can imagine equally bad would be an all-female female – cringing and one hundred per cent passive!

I know little about psychology, but everyday experience has taught me that whatever the advantages (and they are many) of being in a close and loving relationship with another person or persons, none of us (in the meantime) is only a half-person. (I happen to believe that our wholeness depends upon our relationship to God, but that's a different question.)

What does all this suggest about the 'nature' of God? If nothing more, it means we should take care to include 'female attributes' in our idea of God. Catholic reverence for the Virgin Mary acknowledges this insight and helps to preserve an essential balance. Our images and thought-forms may differ, but they should convey the same ultimate truth. God is not 'it'. God is at least all that we understand by personality. (If we take Trinity Sunday seriously, God is more – God is personality-in-relationship.) I find it convenient and comforting to follow the example of Jesus and think of God foremost as 'heavenly father', combining the notions of holiness and fatherhood. But I do not interpret that wonderful insight narrowly.

6 If our words have any validity, God is he/she.

*Saturday 7 September*

A young vagrant shuffled aimlessly past the house this morning in the rain. His jeans were soaked, but he made a cheery remark about the dismal weather. If I *really* cared for people, and if I was *really* committed (before all else) to the service of humanity, I would have invited him into the house for a drink and a warm. But I didn't. With a family to consider, I can scarcely introduce wet vagrants into the home at point blank range. Besides, with sermons to prepare, etc. etc., and buses to drive, I haven't the time, etc. etc. My excuses, though distasteful even to me, are unassailable. But a priest who lived in the city in an easily accessible spot, and who kept open house, could fulfil an important role in the church's mission. He would need few ties, and would need probably to be unmarried. It would be a ministry of great costliness.

Two of us drove coaches to Great Yarmouth this evening, and spent three hours walking round the town while our passengers saw a show. The other driver and I had not previously spoken much together, but after this shift we knew each other better.

It was a rough night, with gale-force winds blowing off-shore. We walked out in the blackness to the end of the pier and watched the sea. As the waves surged towards the beach they were met by the gale which tried in vain to force them back into the deep. And as the waves broke they were seized roughly by the wind, and whipped into clouds of stinging spray which lashed back into our faces. We gripped the rail of the pier tightly, and perhaps were foolish to stand there so exposed: but we were mesmerized by the intensity of the elements. The powerful, relentless swell of the sea; the hysterical anger of the shrieking wind which snatched away our breath – these held us captive. And in the darkness – thrown violently one moment, gliding gracefully the next – we caught white glimpses of gulls who cared nothing for the weather. It was the sea and the wind (more, even, than the tea and the fish and chips) which brought two comparative strangers together. (Later, he spoke of his pal in the army who was killed in Aden.)

Before we left, the moon broke through the cloud and we walked a short distance along the beach. I found the moonlight shining on the heaving water inexpressibly moving. Again, for a few moments, I was held utterly spellbound.

*Sunday 8 September*

I am always pleased to discover a hymn tune which I have overlooked. It doesn't happen very often, but today I found 'Alleluia', by S. S. Wesley.

I was cheered by a delightful spoonerism in the vestry prayer this evening. The steward gave thanks for the hour of worship, which enabled us to turn aside from the bus and rustle of everyday life.

*Monday 9 September*

This was an important day because I started working with a new conductor. I become mildly paranoiac whenever I am faced with a change of conductor; it is a moment of crisis for a crew driver. With a good mate the job is enjoyable, but to be unevenly yoked is hell. I was fortunate again this time. My new conductor is twenty, and his three burning passions seem to be railways, beer and football. We should be able to communicate. Working with someone who has not had time to become old and staid is a powerful antidote to the inertia of middle age. If I spend long in the company of certain mature adults I die a thousand deaths: no zest, no imagination – only moans and groans. In the words of John Wesley: 'To have persons at my ear fretting and murmuring at everything is like tearing the flesh off my bones. I see God sitting upon his throne, and ruling all things well.'

We received an unexpected bonus on our very first trip. A man came running for the bus, obviously having leapt from his bed only minutes before. He was dressing as he hurried up the road, but to our delight had neglected to button his flies. Suddenly, he became aware of this oversight (it was a cold morning). To see him nonchalantly trying to do up his fly buttons while chasing for the bus (I was revving the engine to encourage him) was a splendid start, both to the week and to our partnership!

I am fortunate to live in the city, almost at the gates of the cathedral, and I am able to attend choral evensong frequently. I count this one of the most precious of the many privileges I have been given; I could no longer live without English church music.

From this evening's psalms:

*We wait for thy loving-kindness, O God: in the midst of thy temple.*
*But no man may deliver his brother: nor make agreement unto God for him; for it cost more to redeem their souls . . .*

Tonight I spoke at the local Epilepsy Club.

*Tuesday 10 September*

This is our early week, and we started today at 5.55. As I walked to work I paused on the bridge to admire the cathedral spire, silhouetted dramatically in the sunrise.

In the seclusion of my cab I sing constantly! This morning it was Stanford's 'Te Deum in B flat' – over and over again. ('B flat? You can say that again!' – Roy, my conductor.)

I am able to attend evensong most regularly on early weeks. From the psalms:

*We took sweet counsel together: and walked in the house of God as friends.*

*Wednesday 11 September*

Sitting in the canteen this morning I concluded that writing this journal is a ridiculous exercise – a pointless attempt at self-justification which is bound to fail. Beside me, a card-school was in full swing; and every few moments there were shouts of 'Stop swearing – you'll upset Jack!' and 'Jack, tell him to watch his language – he's a bad influence on me!' and 'Sorry, Jack – there, now he's made me start!' How can the warm and total acceptance to which this good-natured banter testifies be conveyed in writing? It is this I treasure most; it is this, above all, I would have you glimpse. For there are no short-cuts to such acceptance. It is earned only by being there; simply that – morning and night, earlies and lates, summer and winter, in good times and in bad: and by being linked in that final act of identification – economically.

But I will write a little more!

*Thursday 12 September*

Officially this was my rest day, but I was glad to work it; I need the money. I had an interesting conversation with the Union branch secretary – a staunch Labour supporter, straight as a die. He told me he used to regard himself as a communist. He was 'converted' not by Hungary or Czechoslovakia but by the notorious television programme *TW3*! He enjoyed that show so much he soon concluded he could not live happily under a system where such freedom and irreverence was not permitted.

Hospital visit, then evensong.

*God be merciful unto us, and bless us: and shew us the light of his coun-*

*Friday 13 September*
This morning I heard a good bus story with a typical 'Norfolk' flavour. Sometime in the 1930s a bus was going up Westlegate – then a narrow thoroughfare – and met a farm cart. There wasn't room for them to pass. With an air of exasperation the old farmer exclaimed: 'You *know* I come down here *every* Thursday . . .!'

*Saturday 14 September*
A beautiful late-summer's day – though I noticed that the leaves on the sycamore and silver birch are beginning to turn. Steve took a coach to Fakenham Races. He trained as a jockey himself when first he left school – so I gave him five shillings to put on something he fancied. I had never before put money on a horse in my life! (How low can this man stoop?) I know that gambling is trusting in luck and therefore cannot be reconciled with faith in God's loving providence; and I know it is hypocrisy for anyone with socialist leanings to gamble, for the collection of many small sums and their chance distribution to a few is diametrically opposed to all he stands for. But momentarily these seemed very big sticks with which to beat a five shilling flutter at Fakenham. Steve did well. I won two bob.

Roy and his friend called at my local tonight and bought me one.

*Sunday 15 September*
At the heart of the Christian faith is the belief that the creation is controlled and directed by almighty love. It is love which holds the planets in orbit, and whirls the stars along; love which binds energy into matter, and fashions it into a myriad different shapes and forms; love which draws the snowdrop through the frozen earth; love which scents the lilac; love which paints in hoar-frost; love which draws persons mysteriously into relationship. Love is the key to our existence and to the existence of every new morning. Lady Julian of Norwich put it succinctly: 'Love was his meaning.' The creation throbs with every conceivable gradation of love – from the love of lovers and the love of friends, to the love which (St John says) 'the Father hath bestowed upon us' – the love which brought the saviour from above. No rigid distinctions can be drawn. In creation and in redemption, in our relationships and in our worship – love

 was his meaning.

We ought never to be surprised that human relationships can become confused and complicated, for we are struggling clumsily to reflect the love that made us. We are moved by that love which vibrates through the cosmos and which is the source of every attraction and every affection. Whenever we attempt consciously to express love, or channel it into a recognizable relationship, we are immediately restricted by the pathetic inadequacies of our physical and mental apparatus. For love is not sentimentality. Love is not a sweet and cosy emotion. Love is unmanageable. That is why it is so frightening – more frightening than a storm, more frightening than nuclear energy, more frightening than any power known to man.

Love cannot be controlled. Love cannot be compelled. It releases us from the tyranny of reason, only to imprison us helplessly in a new bondage – bitter-sweet, terrible, wonderful. You cannot be ordered to love; you cannot be forced to stop loving. Perhaps it is unrequited love which illustrates most dramatically the awesome, defenceless, persistency of love, enduring the agony of total rejection and never wavering. Love is fearsome. And this is the power that holds all things together.

Christianity is not a code of conduct. It does not mean simply being polite to aunts and kind to animals. Christianity is exposure to love – exposure to this power more searing than any radiation. It does not involve learning a list of rules. It involves laying oneself open to God who is love, recognizing that love is the beginning and the end, believing that 'this is the famous stone that turneth all to gold', accepting that love may throw your attitudes and values upside down, and yielding to the worst that love may do. Love was his meaning. Love is his nature. And Love is his name.

*Monday 16 September*

This was a full but fairly typical day. My routine varies, and has to be built round the shift I am scheduled to work. Today's duty was a split shift, or 'spreadover', and my programme was (approximately) as follows: Up at 6; 7–11 work; 11–1 reading/typing; 1–2 dinner and *The Times*; 2–3 three hospital visits (one church, two bus – fitter's widow; driver's sister-in-law); 3–7 work; then tea, followed by more reading/typing, and a period of prayer and silence in St Clement's. Late this evening I persuaded myself that I had earned a pint.

*Tuesday 17 September*

I drove a school-bus this morning – to my old school. The uniform is the same, but the boys are different: much more precocious. With perfect naturalness, they made remarks to me which I would not have dreamed of making to an adult. They sang strange pop-songs that had no melody; they clapped and shouted football-crowd type slogans; it was all very alien.

The sub-culture to which my generation belonged has given way to another. I can speak with youngsters easily, but it is no longer as one of them. Now I must communicate across a generation gap. I've seldom had this feeling so acutely; I'm getting old!

At the football match tonight my attention was divided between the game and the many moths attracted by the floodlights. Some were very large – clearly hawk-moths.

*Wednesday 18 September*

It was a glorious sunny morning, with a strong hint of autumn in the air. I walked on the edge of the heath, and looked out over the city. Autumn affects my metabolism, and disturbs my brain. I can sense its approach, like the swallows now congregating on the wires. With the mountain-ash berries, the cool, clear mornings, the shortening evenings, and the mere suggestion of mist, a mood of melancholy comes upon me, and a restlessness which, each year, is never assuaged. I wander through the old burial-ground in the late afternoon sunshine and think profound, disturbing thoughts which defy capture and elucidation. I feel sad and stimulated. Autumn is painful and beautiful. I resign myself to loneliness and total loss, yet long for understanding and clearer insight – long to capture and distil the truth behind the dew lying heavy on the grass and shrubs. And this morning I could feel the mood beginning; autumn is all but here. In this season I was born. One day its tantalizing, haunting beauty will break my heart.

I felt another sharp twinge this evening. I drove the bus towards Norwich along the Old Yarmouth Road just as the sun was setting over Filby Broad. I wanted to stop and stare until nightfall. Unfortunately, I had a full standing load! (It's Yarmouth Races this week!) Further along the road I noticed the sunshine beaming between some trees and bushes, bathing everything in gold: even the air looked gold. I'd heard the phrase 'golden sunshine' many times, but never been so aware of it.

This day was simply over-burdened with beauty. I must try not to keep writing about the weather, but sunshine is like bread: we never tire of it; it is part of the framework of life, and it is good.

*Thursday 19 September*

A young conductor to whom I've scarcely spoken jumped on my bus and exclaimed: 'A quick absolution, please!'

He insisted on giving me a definition: A nun is – a bird of pray. He'd saved that one specially for me.

*Friday 20 September*

Today I spent an hour in Ely cathedral – a magnificent pile, very dear to me.

Several commodities have been in short supply in the shops recently, and housewives have been blamed for 'panic buying'. I was delighted to hear of a shop in Soham with a notice in the window: PANIC BUY HERE.

Back to Norwich for evensong:

*He maketh his angels spirits: and his ministers a flaming fire.*

*Saturday 21 September*

A hard shift – and it rained all day. When we arrived at the university we found a large banner announcing the Annual Congress of the BVA. Roy was puzzled by the initials.

'British . . . Association . . .' he mused.

'What about the V?' I asked.

'Victuallers?' he ventured, hopefully.

'No!' I yelled. 'Try Veterinary.'

'Wh-a-a-t – Horse-doctors?'

One or two delegates gave us old-fashioned glances.

*Sunday 22 September*

Perhaps it is easier for those who do not have to bear heavy responsibility, or whose intellectual ability is limited, to maintain their personal integrity and a calm, contented spirit. (I'm not totally convinced by that reasoning; there seems a flaw in it, somewhere.) But whatever the explanation, invariably I have found that the people whose Christian discipleship has impressed me most have not been ecclesiastical power-possessing beings, but simple souls such as the world overlooks: old countrywomen and the like, whose names are known to only a few.

I was privileged to be with one today. In his eighties, he has lived in an institution for nearly fifty-five years. He has attended the same tiny chapel for fifty years, and been the organist for over forty. Few are the services he has missed; for him there have been no holidays. I suspect that all his belongings fit into one locker, but he has other riches – a sweet and gentle and peaceable spirit which stems from his trust in Jesus Christ. ('He was not a superstar,' he told me indignantly one day. 'He was a man of sorrows.') People like this rebuke and inspire me simultaneously. This dear old friend, (who always offers me his tobacco tin), reminds me of Tom Pinch in *Martin Chuzzlewit*. I honour him. I preach to him, but am not in the same class.

In my 'church gear' on the way home I met Roy and three of his friends. They hailed me loudly from across the street, and undaunted by my appearance dragged me (protesting feebly) into a pub. There, for half-an-hour, we had a first-class religious discussion on spiritual healing and the authority of the Bible. They started it.

*Monday 23 September*

There's a certain intensity about life on the buses. We work hard (on irregular shifts) and – to coin a phrase – we laugh hard. It was raining again this morning. Suddenly, Roy and I (in the same instant) spied a woman hurrying through the busy street hugging – of all things – a stuffed badger! We caught each other's eye, and laughed uncontrollably. Perhaps it was a reaction to the miserable morning, but for a time it seemed the funniest thing we had ever seen. Had it been tucked under her arm it might, perhaps, have looked less amusing – but she clutched it determinedly to her bosom, and her glare defied anyone to risk a remark. Knowing there is a right way and a wrong way of doing everything, we wondered what protocol was involved in carrying stuffed badgers correctly.

*Tuesday 24 September*

'Festal Evensong with Procession and Te Deum for the Festival of the Dedication of the Cathedral Church' was rich and satisfying.

*I was glad when they said unto me: We will go into the house of the Lord.*

I try to read one worthwhile book each month; today I finished *The Lost Girl* by D. H. Lawrence (of whom more later).

*Wednesday 25 September*

*Thy hands have made me and fashioned me: O give me understanding, that I may learn thy commandments.*

Ernie is one of my pub-flock. He is a large, uncomplicated, and classic example of a type of Norfolk countryman. In his time he has had the odd brush with the law, and made us laugh tonight as he recounted one such incident. Ernie had occasion, one dark evening, to enter premises which (very unreasonably) had been locked. Ever equal to the occasion, Ernie produced the necessary equipment and sawed the lock out of the door. Thereafter his business was soon completed, and he hurried home to bed. He was awakened late the next morning when two policemen entered his bedroom. They were carrying the sawn-out lock, and said, 'Come on! – You might as well admit it! – We found your fingerprints on the lock.' Our hero, only half awake, replied: 'You bleeding liars. I wore gloves.' He was convicted. When our mirth had subsided, Ernie started us off again by adding, thoughtfully: 'I didn't ought to have said that, did I?'

*Thursday 26 September*

I know ten thousand names and a million faces –
Each an individual,
And each one part of me.
Neighbours talking in the street,
Remote in close proximity,
Separate in unity,
Isolated.

A handful only have unique significance –
Whose destinies were caught upon the wave
That threw them, with my own,
Upon the shore.
Singleness of interest,
Mutual history,
Affection.

Rare is the mingling of personality –
Hesitant, then joyfully careless.

Rare the unconditional revealing,
The acceptance in completeness –
Blemish and genius merging in wholeness;
A fusion unreasoned and intuitive –
Uncompelled,
Powerfully compelling;
Barren, yet quivering in creativity;
A flame kindled in spontaneity,
Shyly nourished upon daring truth,
Fanned into dependence –
Sexual-spiritual, physical-mental, shameless.
A giving and receiving in reciprocity,
Enriching
Through the reaction of contrast and similarity,
And proved in silence.

*Friday 27 September*

I'm afraid I don't always sing English church music in the cab. Today, on the third wet morning rush-hour this week, a car driven by an old man cut sharply in front of me, and I swore loudly. Then I noticed that my bus was one used for driver-instruction, with a removable glass panel behind me. It was ill-fitting (I had wondered where the draught was coming from) and I was afraid in case someone had heard me.

Tonight in the pub Roy complained about the *War Cry*. 'I started reading an article about football, and it's turned into an article about religion.'

*Saturday 28 September*

It rained during part of the football match this afternoon (we beat Manchester United 2–0), and there was a good rainbow. The second goal was a beauty. The United supporters were giving former United player Ted MacDougall some stick, chanting continually 'MacDougall is a reject.' Suddenly, he latched on to the ball and it hit the back of the net like a cannon-shot. The chanting stopped dead.

Roy asked if it was difficult to find sermon subjects: 'But surely there's an *Observer's Book of Sermons* . . .?'

'No, there isn't!' I snapped.

*Sunday 29 September*

Michaelmas – the feast of St Michael the Archangel and All Angels. The michaelmas daisies are making a seasonable splash of colour in the garden.

This evening I preached in the village chapel where at the age of sixteen I delivered my first address from a pulpit. I made good friends that night – a farmer and his wife and son, who gave me a gift beyond price. They invited me to visit their farm whenever I wished, and in so doing they reinforced my awareness of the earth and the seasons, which even then was alert and sensitive. Now I had fields over which I could tramp, farm-sheds through which I could wander, bullocks I could feed, countrymen to whose conversation I could stand in a corner and listen.

I had tea at the farm today. It is small and unpretentious, and I love being there. I buried the farmer's wife two years ago. She never realized how much she had given me, though often I tried to tell her.

*Monday 30 September*

The young conductor who defined nuns for me the other day taught me another 'religious' joke this morning, which involved folding and tearing a piece of paper in a certain manner to produce a cross and the letters HELL.

A bus passed me slowly this afternoon (travelling in the opposite direction) with the hands of the driver clasped together devoutly in an attitude of prayer! It is these trivial gestures which are the hallmark of genuine acceptance.

I spent part of this evening with a teenager who, from completely outside the life of the church, is considering studying for the priesthood. Another friend was ordained priest yesterday. I have been very critical of the church, and of the ministry in particular; my present mode of existence is a prophetic demonstration against modern, middle-class, out-of-touch Christianity. But Christ and his church are everything to me, and always I am moved by the idealism and faith which takes a man into the ministry of the church of God.

*Tuesday 1 October*

This morning I spoke to a fifth-form class at my old school.

God is at once 'knowable' and utterly elusive; through faith in Christ I have found confidence and hope – yet each day I long to see more clearly.

*Wednesday 2 October*

A day of memories. On this corresponding Wednesday last year I was responsible for calling a one-day strike which took every bus off the streets of Norwich, and also left a large area of the county without public transport.

If you were asked to name the costliest gift you had ever given, you might find the question difficult, even embarrassing. I would answer like a shot: the two years I served as branch chairman of the Union. It wasn't just the extra meetings I had to attend (though I have made clear already my aversion to meetings). Much worse was the impossibility of having a quiet cup of tea in the canteen without somebody having a question to raise, or the very real possibility of meeting a brother in the darkened streets on the way to work at 6 a.m. whose morning greeting would be, 'Ah, I've been waiting to see you . . .' – and who would then proceed to enunciate a list of grievances. I found this constant obligation to talk shop extremely wearisome, especially when so many of the complaints were fatuously trivial.

Chairing the monthly committee meetings was an important duty, requiring a light rein in a grip of steel. Everybody was given an equal opportunity to contribute to the discussions – but if anyone trespassed on the prerogatives of the chair or tried to usurp the position of the chairman, he was given short shrift. I saw the first responsibility of the office to be that of holding my team together – rather like a minister in a church. On issues where the team were divided, I remained the chairman of each faction, and my duty was to lead and unite.

If the committee meetings could be tough, branch meetings could be terrifying! Usually the attendance at these meetings is small, but when an issue has packed the hall with angry men it takes a special kind of determination to stand up on the platform, look round slowly and deliberately, and begin: 'Brothers . . .' The conduct of the branch meeting is an acid test of the credibility of a chairman. It isn't easy to call a man sharply to order and still maintain a good relationship with him, doing it in such a spirit that he is not humiliated, and made resentful. Good humour is part of the secret – but it's not easy to be good humoured when people are trying to crucify you. Branch meetings are not like devotional evenings.

I enjoyed presenting the disciplinary appeals of our members. Life is too short! I have always fancied a career at the (legal!) bar, and this part of the job gave me an opportunity to practice my homespun variety of do-it-yourself advocacy. Confronted by one who saw himself as a second Birkett or Marshall Hall, the company had to take more care over disciplinary matters! Sometimes they were very bad. In one case a boy was sacked for unsatisfactory driving when it was plain to everyone that really he was being sacked because his hair was long and the company objected. They muddled their case so much that in the end I had to deliver a strike ultimatum to expedite a reasonable settlement. (I regarded dismissal appeals as my capital murder cases!) The number of successful appeals increased gradually to a respectable proportion, giving our members slightly more faith in the system. 

Only rarely did I take a decision without first consulting with members of my committee, though on the few occasions when a snap decision was required and no committee members were to hand, I was not afraid to give an immediate (and final) answer to the company. One such decision caused an uproar among the members, but I had given a verdict and it could not be undone. At that period I experienced most keenly the loneliness of intense opposition and bitter animosity. There was nothing to do but live through it, and wait until it burned itself out – but it was hard. Earlier, one committee member had been forced to resign after weeks of worrying and a prolonged battering from the ever-questioning brothers had landed him in hospital, perilously close to a nervous breakdown. The pressures are real.

Then came the one-day stoppage. The basic irritant was a drastic and undeniable deterioration in our working conditions, arising from a shortage of buses; this, in turn, was caused by a shortage of fitters and spares. The situation was made virtually impossible for me to control by a series of minor acts of mismanagement: failure to consult; failure to inform; failure to abide by undertakings given. Admittedly, the management was under great pressure at the time, but unfortunately they had forfeited already much of their credibility in the eyes of my committee by a string of careless incidents which had occurred from the beginning of the year. My personal position had been made most difficult by the third failing listed above – neglecting to ensure that things they had told me *would* happen *did* happen. When I repeated the assurances of the management to my members, only to find – in the event – the very opposite happening, my own credibility (and that of my committee) was imperilled. I did not like that.

In a noisy meeting, my exasperated committee (who were taking a daily hammering) threw at me all these matters. I listened carefully. On similar occasions the secretary and I had counselled restraint. (The company will never know how much they owed us.) This time, however, the list was too long and too convincing.

There was no point asking for yet another meeting with the management; temporarily, we felt we couldn't rely on their assurances. With great reluctance, I concluded that they must be given a short, sharp lesson. I asked my committee if they felt a one-day strike might make the point that the Union had to be taken seriously. That was exactly how they felt. A special branch meeting was called for the Sunday morning following, and it was to a packed hall that I spoke from the chair: 'Now collectively you may be prepared to be treated in this way,' I thundered, 'but I am not prepared to be treated like this on your behalf.' They loved it. I spoke for twenty-five minutes. The atmosphere was not unlike a revival meeting! A taste of chapel oratory was a spiritual treat for them! With the waverers convinced, I sat down to loud applause and the strike was on. I vacated the chair during 'Any Other Business' to perform a quick change and dash off to conduct the harvest festival! I left the hall to renewed cheers.

At the end of the morning service I found the branch committee waiting self-consciously at the church door, and we held a strike-committee meeting in the vestry. They were more alert than I had ever seen them, and the secretary formally and generously thanked me for my speech. The next few days contained plenty of work and worry, but the strike was one hundred per cent. I thus became one of the few clergymen in the country to do picket duty.

It cost us a day's pay – but it achieved all we intended. After the strike only a few weeks of my office remained. The two years had been a unique experience, throughout which I relied greatly on my secretary (who was also in office for the first time). Slightly younger than I, he was particularly impressive in the negotiating committee meetings with top management and had the agreement at his fingertips. Neither of us intended to cling to office at any price, and therein lay our strength. Anyone who thought he could do the job better (and could convince the brothers accordingly) would have been able to replace either of us easily. One vote of no confidence would have been enough; but nobody tried. We made a good team because we trusted and supported each other, and played it straight. We took no nonsense from the branch; the agreement might be amended, but it would not be ridden over rough-shod while we held office. By the same token, we took no nonsense from the company. I thought it was almost a priestly role. Certainly, we concluded, life might well have been easier on all sides if we had shown more 'flexibility'. (Note the inverted commas; I am talking about integrity, not rigidity.) That was not the way we chose; and for that I honour him. We gave the brothers strong leadership. There aren't many thanks. You're a fool if you expect them.

I didn't stand for re-election, although after the strike I would have expected to have been returned comfortably. How ironic! Only a few weeks before, my personal decision in that one particular incident had made me acutely unpopular. It's best to treat praise and disgrace in much the same way: with the least drama possible. They follow each other quickly.

Anyone worth his salt can do two jobs – in my case, buses and church. The Clydeside MP, Jimmy Maxton, said once: 'If you can't ride two horses at once you shouldn't be in the bloody circus at all.' But when a third responsibility was added I began to struggle. To have survived those two years was a near-miracle (for there were so many other things I enjoyed doing, too). I helped to steer the branch through a difficult period, and having tidied up a few matters, I retired and left it to others. I am thrilled most by the fact that, far from impairing personal relationships with the brothers and with management (which had been my great fear), my term of office enlarged and enhanced them. And they still recognize me as a minister. As the boy said: 'You're a bloody nice bloke, but as a union man you're fucking useless.' But that was before the strike!

*Thursday 3 October*

I attended the short Judge's Service – formerly the Assize Service – at the cathedral. I enjoy seeing the civic coach, the city regalia, the colourful robes, the choir and processional cross, the copes of the canons; I am captivated by the organ voluntaries and the fanfares of trumpets. In our sophisticated society, time-honoured traditions and ceremonies tend – like some of our finest old buildings – to vanish overnight. If it is inevitable, it is also much to be deplored. A sense of historic continuity can be a source of great pleasure and personal enrichment, and a touch of ceremonial adds colour to our way of life which, for all our affluence, seems paradoxically to be growing strangely drab and uniform. I believe there are practical benefits, too, which tend to be under-estimated. I remember seeing the Assize judges being driven to the station one Friday afternoon to catch the London train. They were wearing pin-striped trousers and hard-hats – and I would have answered back to them with impunity. 'Good,' say the reformers, 'they are only men.' But I am not sure it is such a bad thing to have a certain awe for the law and those who represent and embody it. No law, no civilized society; and most people known to me would think twice before showing open contempt towards a red judge. His appearance gives him an initial (and proper) advantage. I like to see High Court judges in scarlet and ermine; bishops in mitres; lord mayors in black and gold, with chains of office. We have left so little that passes as pageantry we should be slow to relinquish that which remains, be it civic, ecclesiastical, or judicial.

This afternoon I conducted the funeral service of a bus conductor whose sudden death was a great shock. Representatives of both union and management were present.

Evensong:

*With the holy thou shalt be holy: and with a perfect man thou shalt be perfect.*

*With the clean thou shalt be clean: and with the froward thou shalt learn frowardness.*

*Friday 4 October*

Today I was filmed driving a bus in the station yard, and interviewed in the canteen for a religious television programme. I was so careful to re-enter the world quietly and unobtrusively six years ago that I suffer agonies of self-consciousness, even now, at this kind of fuss. When the television lights were fitted up I was horrified. I think, however, I need not have bothered. If this had been my first week at work I would have been in trouble; but I have more than served my apprenticeship. My colleagues may even look for something like this occasionally; they watched with noisy interest, and some seemed to derive a vicarious prestige out of the attention given to me! But still I was glad when it was over.

*Saturday 5 October*

The trees along Riverside Road are ablaze with shades of copper, bronze and gold.

Each season of the year has its distinctive beauty and attractiveness. Spring and autumn – the seasons of change – are my favourites, with May and October the months I enjoy most. Summer has the long, bright days, the trees in full foliage, warmth and holidays. Spring has bulbs and bursting buds, singing birds, new life, and all the joy of Easter. Winter brings the exquisite artistry of the hoar-frost, and the perfectly-designed snowflake, and the excitement of Christmas and New Year. But it is autumn that touches me most deeply. Nature seems to have one last fling before the sleep of winter. Gardens and hedges provide a riot of colour in leaf and berry, flower and fruit. There is mist in the morning, and smoke from garden bonfires; the sunshine is mellow and casts long shadows, and as the nights pull in and we feel a nip in the air we can start lighting fires again. It is, of course, a season with an essential touch of sadness, a solemnity amid the gaiety, a hint of death. Among the days in the church calendar are All Saints' Day and All Souls' Day which – with Remembrance Day – seem to blend perfectly with the spirit of the season.

The harvest festival services at the beginning of each autumn reflect the deep impulse (which comes to us from ages long past) to offer gifts and tokens of gratitude for the fertility and bounty of the earth. Instinctively, we feel it is 'a joyful and pleasant thing' to be thankful. The harvest hymns, the sight and smell of the decorated church, the message of thankfulness – these are reminders of the fields and the sea and the sky.

When I was a minister in Glasgow, surrounded by grey tenement blocks and filthy back courts (and wonderful people), I scarcely noticed the seasons change. I had no garden; no leaves fell in the street in autumn because there were no trees. Only when I passed the park did I notice – *really* notice – what time of the year it was. I think that is an illustration of something disastrous which is happening in our civilization. We are losing our awareness of the natural order and our place in it. We are cutting ourselves off, in our modern, hectic, urban civilization, from a daily awareness of the round of the seasons, from solstice and equinox, from the planets. The glare of the city-lights blots out the stars in their constellations. I find this not merely sad, but deeply, depressingly disturbing. (If this is all poetic nonsense, I'm sorry; but I think it goes deeper than that.)

During my three years in the Fens – those flat, fertile lands where the horizon is usually visible on every side – often I used to walk alone by the river. I remember vividly walking late one winter afternoon from Brandon Bank to Brandon Creek along the high bank of the Little Ouse. One farmer had been ploughing, and the freshly-turned, jet-black Fen soil looked good and wholesome, and I would have run my fingers through it had I not been on my way to visit an old sick man. The sun had dropped out of a clear sky and the first stars soon became visible, and a keen, frosty wind bit into my face and made me pull my coat-collar higher. Another farmer had been threshing peas, and huge bonfires of shells and stalks were dotted across one field like ancient beacons, with flames leaping high into the air as night came on. Beside me, the river flowed swiftly with its own secret life, and a solitary swan paid little attention to me.

There they were – earth, air, fire, water: the four primary elements. And suddenly I became aware of them, and felt myself to be in a conjunction with them, in a close and vital and intimate relationship: alone with them, connected to them, part of them. It was a vivid, spiritual experience, at once soothing, renewing, invigorating, tantalizing, because it awakened sensations and aspirations I knew not how to satisfy. To return to the car and drive home seemed like a denial, an abdication, an unspeakable loss. Not all spiritual experiences occur in church. I do not know that I was a better man for that experience, but I believe I somehow became larger and, I hope, wiser. I cannot put it more clearly.

But men are losing it – and I am fearful. It is a loss which leads not only to a profound personal impoverishment, but to a definite proneness to abuse the creation. Just as men – if they refuse to love each other – will kill each other, so if we refuse to befriend the creation we will tarnish it. In the canteen at work a few days ago a man said to me: 'I think one of the saddest sights in the world is a dead river.' I agreed wholeheartedly. People think the river which flows through Norwich looks cheerless as they peer at it from the window when the bus goes over the bridge – but it isn't! It's alive! There are water-weeds and yellow lillies; there are perch and pike; there are ducks and swans and moorhens. If you were up in the morning early you might even catch sight of a kingfisher. It's a living river. But go to the Midlands, or up North, and see a dead river – murky, oiled, polluted, empty, evil-looking, stinking. It is a fearsome experience. The further we stray from a vivid awareness of our part in a living creation, the more we become disposed to pollute and corrupt the creation. Already we have made an alarming beginning, using the seas as a dump; poisoning the atmosphere with radio-active fall-out; killing our wild-life with pesticides; destroying landscapes with careless planning; choking cities with diesel fumes; ripping up hedgerows; hunting creatures like the whale until their very survival as a species is threatened.

Recently, a hippie-type friend showed me a ring he had placed on his wedding-finger. 'Man,' he said to me, 'I am married to the creation. When I see a tree I say, "Tree, I love you." When I look up at the sky I say, "Stars, I love you." When I stoop down and touch the ground I say, "Earth, I love you. I promise I will try never to abuse you in any way." ' I confess I found that a beautiful and meaningful (if unorthodox) concept.

If anyone says we've to 'get back to nature' we think he means we should live in rabbit holes on the heath, and eat blackberries. Nothing so drastic is called for. But we have become incredibly blasé about the astonishing universe in which we find ourselves, and many of us have lost our sense of wonder and mystery. It is a terrible loss. Try to visit the coast in winter and gaze at the sea; find time to look at the stars, and take the trouble to pick out the constellations; see the gardening as more than a burden! These are, potentially, deeply religious activities which can help to restore that ancient harmony, and strengthen the spirit.

*Monday 7 October*

At the terminus we watched a kestrel hovering.

Evensong:

*Commit thy way unto the Lord, and put thy trust in him: and he shall bring it to pass.*

One of the great secrets of life is to recognize one's happiness and to be grateful for it *at the time* – not to look back, years later, and admit sadly: 'I was happy then, and never knew it.' I am happy, and grateful for every day. (Joyful is a better word than happy.)

It was a shock tonight to realize that I had filled a nineteen-hour day. It was an effortless mixture of work and play and worship: early shift; in the study this afternoon; evensong; a driver brought his record collection round this evening; I finished up in the pub with another friend. Add to these things my home and family, and you will see I am rich indeed. And I know it.

*Tuesday 8 October*

I watched a family of house-martins swooping in and out of their mud nest; their cries were loud, and they seemed restless and uneasy. At any moment – when the signal is given – they will begin their long flight south. Not for them 'the exquisite artistry of the hoar-frost, and the perfectly-designed snowflake'!

*Like as the hart desireth the water brooks: so longeth my soul after thee, O God.*

If it is simply and vividly presented, history – especially church history – possesses a quality of inspiration to which many types of people respond. Two years ago in the parish church I gave a lecture to some university students; at the end, to my surprise, they began to applaud – then became inhibited, not sure if it was correct procedure to applaud clerical gentlemen on consecrated ground! I was reminded of this incident tonight when I gave another long lecture to a men's group on 'The Origins of Wesleyan and Primitive Methodism, with special reference to Methodism in Norwich'. As usual, the meeting closed with a hymn and I suggested 'The Primitive Methodist Grand March': 'Hark! the Gospel news is sounding'. I was astonished once more! The lecture had evoked a powerful atmosphere, and my listeners spontaneously sang the first verse of the hymn over again at the end – something rarely experienced these days! Church history is indeed, in Bishop Creighton's words, 'a cordial for drooping spirits'.

*Wednesday 9 October*

I hurried from work in time to speak at the church fellowship.

'God makes it very hard for us to be chaste' (quotation of the day!).

*Thursday 10 October*

It is remarkable how a vivid dream can determine the flavour of an entire day. It keeps flashing back into the consciousness, and one is ever expecting to meet the person most intimately involved.

I admired the graceful lines of a group of horses sheltering from the rain, under some trees.

Here we are at the terminus again; we turn, and go back . . .

General Election. Voted.

*Friday 11 October*

*O set me up upon the rock that is higher than I: for thou hast been my hope, and a strong tower for me against the enemy.*

I learnt another hymn tune: 'Beulah', by G. M. Garrett, to which is sung 'There is a land of pure delight'.

I have four unorthodox patron saints, among whom is Edith Piaf; this was the eleventh anniversary of her death. The genius of Edith Piaf stemmed from the incredible twists of fortune which fashioned her extraordinary life. The drama of her birth was simply a foretaste of the dramas which were to follow: she was born in the early hours of 19 December 1915, and was delievered by two gendarmes while her father had gone to summon an ambulance. She was named after Edith Cavell, who had recently been shot by the Germans in Belgium (and who is buried beside Norwich cathedral).

Thereafter, her life was a unique blend of hope, misery, success, poverty, affluence, and *l'amour*. Alcoholism, drug-addiction, major operations, scandal, shattering bereavements – all these formed part of her lot. To many she was an open example of moral degradation, but her genius was irresistable and undeniable – an expression of the blows and caresses that life had dealt her. Songs like 'La Vie en Rose' and 'Hymne à l'amour' utterly nullified the complexities of morality when sung by Piaf, and spoke with immediacy and authenticity.

Throughout her life she loved, and searched for love – but disillusionment seemed always to be waiting round the corner. Two of her greatest songs were recorded towards the end of her life: 'Milord' in 1959, and 'Non, je ne regrette rien' in 1960. In failing health and – characteristically – in the face of wagging tongues, she married Théo Sarapo, a singer twenty years her junior, in October 1962. They were allowed one year together before that astonishing voice was stilled for ever.

To me, the life of Edith Piaf illustrates what it means to be a human being. I honour her for the sheer power and emotional appeal of her singing; I am awed by her courage. Her life demonstrates also the fundamental truth that we have to accept people as they are, not as we would like them to be. When we can do this with sincerity, often we are greatly surprised. People become more agreeable and more gifted than ever we could have imagined; then we are all made richer.

*Saturday 12 October*

Norwich cathedral from Riverside Road must be one of the most noble views in England. This afternoon, the colourful rugger-jerseys on the grammar school playing-field and the autumnal tints in the

trees enhanced the scene. How fortunate I am to drive past here many times each week! Always I steal a quick, appreciative glance – and never tire of what I see.

*Sunday 13 October*

I have been drawing parallels and thinking about the different ways in which people and property become lost. Most items are *lost outside*, and the resultant distress is familiar even to the smallest child. Amid the pressures of living in a world of unprecedented speed, change, and anxiety, many people have become lost. They have lost all sense of purpose or direction, lost their values and standards, lost their faith in the love of God, lost their idealism, lost their hope, lost their sense of wonder. Christ can restore our perspective. He is the source of all wonder, hope, idealism, faith, lasting values, and purposefulness.

Some things are *lost inside*: the coin which slips from your pocket and disappears down the side of the armchair is lost; not lost outside, not lost far away – but lost nonetheless! It is possible to be within the fellowship of the church and to be lost. Over-familiarity with holy things; a faith inherited unquestioningly from parents and friends; the inability to see the wood for the trees. Yet in the church's worship, fellowship, and eucharist, Christ is in contact with us, and is waiting to break through.

You can be *lost without knowing it*. Roy and I went on a country journey with the bus, and thought we knew the way; we took a wrong turn and became lost. We didn't realize what had happened; others suspected because they waited and we didn't arrive. It happens occasionally: only when the road narrows and becomes the drive to a big house, or the lane turns into a cart-track leading to a pond, are suspicions aroused! Thousands are lost without knowing it. Life *seems* to hold together. The weekly routine is rather dull, and it doesn't do to think too much about certain things, but they get by. Sometimes a wistfulness touches them, and a mood come on them – but it passes. They are lost! Where is the sparkle and gaiety of life? Where is the joy? This complacency can be pierced by Christ. He is likely to do it in any number of different ways: a funeral service, a sunset, the look of a friend, a flower, the saying of a child.

You can be *lost and know it, though others don't know it*. Some youngsters on a hill-climbing and map-reading test became hopelessly lost; they were not missed for many hours, and by then were in serious trouble. I wonder how many people we touch in the course of a year (or a week) who know that they are lost. Full of unhappiness and despair, they are searching and longing – yet for what, they are not sure! You and others about them never dream they feel like this ('If only we had *known* . . .') Christ wants you to be not an interfering old busybody, but sensitive and alert and truly sympathetic to these around you. Through you, Christ may be able to reach those who know already that there is a dimension lacking in their lives – the dimension of unity, purpose, love, and truth: the God-dimension. 

You can be *lost in a crowd*; indeed, this can be the loneliest place of all. And if you are supposed to be the life and soul of the party, or the leader of the enterprise, that loneliness can be black. Those who bear burdens and responsibilities deserve our understanding. Surrounded by friends, supporters, and admirers, they can have fears and hopes that weigh heavily upon them.

You can be *lost alone*. To feel isolated, to feel no vital connection with any other human person is a terrible experience more widespread than we suspect. Try to give people time and true feeling. 'It is not good for man to be alone'; that was God's verdict, and all who suffer in this way are dear to him.

It is even possible for something to be *lost deliberately* – like the Christmas gift puppies which become unwanted, and are taken to deserted places and abandoned. Satan deceives and leads astray. The powers of evil seem highly organized and possess diabolical cunning. We appear to be deliberately misled, thwarted, and confused. But we should take heart. The Son of Man is also the strong Son of God, who came to seek and to save that which was lost. His power is greater than any evil force. His power is questing love.

I worked a late shift. The conductor (not Roy) was telling me of a prophecy he had made to his brother which eventually had come true. 'Gosh, he was surprised,' the conductor said, 'he thought I must be sciatic!' I've heard of people being physic, but this was a new one, and I appreciated it!

*Monday 14 October*

I leaned out of the cab today to speak to Terry, aged about twenty, who was a bus conductor until a few months ago. Poetry is one of his great loves, and I used to read his work with interest. 'I've written quite a bit, lately,' he informed me. 'I think it's the changing season – I find always I want to write more in the winter than in the summer.'

*Tuesday 15 October*

My thoughts about being lost came to me during a shift (and finished up as a sermon). Roy provided some of the illustrations, and today he asked: 'What's our subject for next Sunday?'

Here is a different kind of illustration – an example of human friction, which I initiated. Through no fault of ours, we arrived at the school ten minutes late this afternoon. When the boys started pushing to get on the bus, the master on gate-duty sent all of them back to form an orderly queue. I was exasperated beyond words. Certainly, I didn't want them trampled under foot, but they could have been regulated without delaying us further. His schoolmaster's authority looked laughable and his self-importance offensive when displayed on the pavement. 'Come on, mate,' I groaned, 'I'm ten minutes late already.' 'Then you'll have to be a bit later,' he retorted. 'Why, you cheeky so-and-so,' I exclaimed – and it was nearly worse! I've noticed this kind of thing before at school gates: schoolmasters thinking that busmen will wait happily while they show off and proudly chasten the children. I think he should have had the sensitivity to realize that we have a schedule to adhere to. But as a Christian I ought not to have groaned at him; nor called him names.

Another sign of my madness became apparent this evening. It rained hard; in fact, there has been much rain over the past month. But tonight, for some reason, I did not want it to leave off before I finished work at 11.15. I wanted badly to walk home in the rain, and feel it on my face. My wish was granted. (And I was drenched!)

*Wednesday 16 October*

*Mercy and truth are met together: righteousness and peace have kissed each other.*

Most modern office blocks do not impress me – they fill me with alarm and despair. But recently one new building of glass and concrete caught my attention early in the morning when the rising sun filled it with fire, and set it seemingly ablaze. Tonight, I noticed this building had been illuminated. The concrete shone pure white in the surrounding darkness, and looked very effective.

*Thursday 17 October*

Today I was thirty-five. Already I have been given two years more than my Lord. After the recent rain, it was a glorious day; morning mist, sunshine, autumn colours. I decided it was good to be alive, so

I bought a bunch of flowers for my mother and thanked her for having me! In the late afternoon sunshine I saw smoke from some cottage chimneys rising straight into the air. I notice this particularly in the autumn; the sun, low in the sky, highlights the smoke, and the cottages seem homely and inviting. It was also Stephen's birthday, so we took our wives out for a meal. A happy day; I was sorry when it was over.

*Friday 18 October*

It is not always easy to believe. Faith burns brightly some days, but on others the temptation to relinquish faith can grow strong and attractive. Yet if we were to yield, our difficulties would not be over. We might no longer have to defend difficult doctrines, or put into words ideas and concepts for which everyday language seems so inadequate; but new problems would appear to replace the old. For there are two sides to the problem of belief.

Whenever I feel spiritually at a low-ebb, and doubts crowd in upon each other, and I start to wonder whether anything matters very much, it is never long before certain things begin to happen. I see the tall spire of the cathedral, and the masons' superb craftsmanship; I watch the setting sun lighting that spire, and filling the sky in the west with shades of red and pink and orange. I notice beauty and wisdom in the lined face of an aged person; promise in the life of a child; poignancy and grace in the lines of young adulthood (where inexperience and ungainliness are combined wonderfully with eagerness and contagious vigour). I see dew on the lawn and russet shades on the apples. I hear boys singing psalms and carols. I hear stories of self-sacrifice and courage. I sit in a church. I talk with a friend. I see the first snowfall. I watch bread and wine being consecrated. I listen to Mahler's 5th Symphony. I see faces in the bus queue.

These and countless other experiences combine to engender a reverence within me, and evoke a sense of wonder and awe – a marvelling at simply *being*. And I want no 'rational' explanations of these experiences! Now it is the turn of the 'intellectuals' to sound irrelevant and superficial. You see what has happened? There is also a problem of unbelief! You may decide to manage without God the Spirit who moves through the whole creation, touching our lives with love and beauty, and ever calling us to experience his fullness more completely, but you cannot prevent these stirrings in your soul. Unbelief is pierced again and again by love and courage and friendship and beauty and worship and craftsmanship and music and kindness – all of which speak to us direct, without benefit of reasoned explanation. In these ways the creation is shot through with God – with the divine energy which has not only made us for himself, but ordained that our hearts should be restless, until they find their rest in him.

*Saturday 19 October*

Like everyone else, I have days when nothing goes right. It doesn't happen often, but when it does I just resign myself to misunderstanding, rejection, and loneliness; I don't struggle – I wait for something more to go wrong. (Perhaps there is a perverse pleasure in feeling sorry for oneself?) This was my precious rest day, for which I had made careful arrangements; but both the people with whom I had planned to spend part of the day were unable to keep our engagement. That started me off, and I was miserable for the rest of the day. Part of my trouble is too many late nights, too much pub, and not enough prayer.

*Sunday 20 October*

I baptized a bus driver's baby son at the morning service. Another driver and his wife stood as godparents. I enjoy these occasions when church and work are joined.

Late this afternoon I caught a bus to the terminus, just beyond the city boundary, and walked a few miles to a village where I preached at the chapel. It was a pleasant walk: a delicate afterglow, some black clouds climbing from the horizon, a pale quarter-moon, small birds rustling in the hedgerows where they had flown to roost, the hedges themselves full of colour. I pulled my cloak round me, and felt I was on a pilgrimage.

In a sense, I was. This was the village chapel where I was married one hot Midsummer Day; the place seemed full of ghosts and memories. It was one of the last village chapels in the area to succumb to the full blast of modern 'secularism'; that fact has made the transformation of the last fifteen years devastatingly plain, and inescapably significant.

*Monday 21 October*

*Blessed be the Lord God of Israel from everlasting, and world without end: and let all the people say, Amen.*

The observation is made about Ursula Brangwen in D. H. Lawrence's *Women in Love*: 'She lived a good deal by herself . . . *always thinking, trying to lay hold on life, to grasp it in her own understanding.*' The circumstances of our age have manoeuvred us into a false position in which we tend to speak and think about God in that manner. We are so anxious to master our subject (!) and assert the existence of God. We define and describe; we reason and infer; we try to lay hold upon God, and grasp him in our own understanding. How small he would be if he could so easily be captured and circumscribed by mortals. He is not only greater than we think, but greater than we are *capable* of thinking. I hope God may be sensed in the catholicity of these pages: but he will not be cornered! God is chiefly to be enjoyed, not defined.

*Tuesday 22 October*

Virginity and Nonconformity is a poisonous and deadly mixture.

'Nothing human disgusts me, unless it's unkind or violent' (Tennessee Williams, *The Night of the Iguana*).

*Wednesday 23 October*

The alarm clock rang at five. It was a cold, dark morning, and a strong wind was lashing the rain against the window. I wanted desperately to stay in bed, and cursed myself for a fool as I crept through the deserted streets to the garage.

*Not unto us, O Lord, not unto us, but unto thy Name give the praise: for thy loving mercy, and for thy truth's sake.*

This month I have re-read Graham Greene's *The Power and the Glory*, a modern crucifixion story full of deep Christian insight. I have read also *A Little of What You Fancy* – the fifth of H. E. Bates' hilarious stories of the Larkin family, pleasantly sexy and very funny indeed.

*Thursday 24 October*

A large area of farmland on the edge of the city is soon to be turned into a considerable suburb, and a heaviness hangs over the fields. The stubble from the last corn ever to grow there stands forlorn, and the last crop of sugar-beet is being harvested. The fields, hedges, and trees are sad.

I took a wrong turn in the city this morning, and had to go all round the one-way system to put myself right. After four hours on one service, we had switched to another; but automatically I followed the first route. More merriment!

*Make me to understand the way of thy commandments: and so shall I talk of thy wondrous works.*

*Friday 25 October*

We laughed this morning in the canteen when a young conductor recounted a recent experience. He was standing by a bus stop in the city, ready to begin his shift, when he was approached by a foreign gentleman. The conversation went something like this:

'Excuse me. Could you tell me where whore is?'

'What?'

'Could you tell me where whore is? Me want to make love.'

'Wrong time, mate. You want night-time. Dark.'

'No – me want make love now – quickly.'

He produced an address, so the conductor was able to direct him. It's all part of the service.

Evensong included the verse which the choristers sing with an unbecoming relish: 'I have more understanding than my teachers: for thy testimonies are my study.'

Sometimes, I feel it is almost obscene to talk to lonely and unhappy women about the love of God when I know that, in fact, they long for the love of man; or to speak of the purifying fire of the Holy Spirit when I know they need a purging, phallic refinement. There are so many lonely people about.

*Saturday 26 October*

The ancient church of St Clement which stands opposite our house was floodlit tonight for the first time, and presented a picture of pure magic. I simply could not believe our good fortune.

Children remind me of caterpillars – messy, and frequently rather horrible. Adolescence is the equivalent of the pupal stage, when all kinds of astonishing changes are taking place beneath the surface. From this condition – in the middle and late teens – emerge the young adults, miraculously transformed into interesting individuals with personality and opinions. The process is gradual, though swift. I can think of caterpillars I knew five years ago – then aged about twelve – whom I regard now as equals. They are short on experience, but more than compensate with an energy and enthusiasm which has all the beauty and liveliness of a creature freshly emerged. To

realize the change has taken place can be a shock. Without your noticing their arrival, they are there. New people.

I ought, perhaps, to add a postscript. I take children seriously, and don't talk down to them; their 'inequality' relates only to the strength of the burdens they are able to bear.

*Sunday 27 October*

As I would not be able to attend any of my usual services today, I rose early and went to eight o'clock holy communion. Later this morning I attended my Trade Union branch meeting; afterwards, we had a splendid discussion in the bar. I worked a late shift. Summer Time ended today, and it was dark early. A strong, blustery wind plucked at the leaves remaining on the trees; the hunters' moon rode high above the clouds which raced at great speed through the night.

*Monday 28 October*

I sing and I think all day long in my cab. It's a good thing people can't hear me sing. It's even more fortunate they can't read my thoughts. Thank heavens we still can call our thoughts our own; *they*, at least, cannot be taxed, or taken away, or held up to ridicule. If people only knew the things we turned over in our minds! . . . Good Lord! Look at those legs . . . She looks terrific in that uniform; I shouldn't mind . . . '*Lecher!*' . . . That youth stripped to the waist loading bags of potatoes on a farm cart is the most handsome man I can recall seeing . . . That elegant centre-half is very beautiful . . . '*Pervert!*' . . . I wonder what the relationship was between Jesus and Mary Magdalen . . . And between Jesus and St John, the disciple whom Jesus loved . . . '*Blasphemer!*' . . . Religion and sex seem to be linked closely . . . Churchgoing seems sometimes to make people worse than they would be . . . '*Heretic!*' . . . There is so little 'otherness' in church services, and how boring they are . . . I'm dying for a drink . . . '*Hypocrite!*' . . . Why has Jesus such an attraction for me? . . . 'My Jesus I love thee, I know thou art mine' . . . '*Holy Joe!*'

But this goes on behind a facade; all the time; with us all. We put up a front; and nobody is any the wiser. How rarely we truly meet.

*Tuesday 29 October*

At the terminus I saw the empty mud-nest of my house-martins, and wondered where they are now, and if all made the journey safely. I watched a flock of gulls following a plough.

Today, an autumn song I learnt at primary school thirty years ago (and have never forgotten) kept running through my head. The simple tune captured the mood of the season perfectly with the peace and gentle finality of a benediction; and these – as I remember them – were the words:

> Goodnight, Goodnight, my children
> Says kindly Father Sun,
> For Summer's days are ended
> Her work is almost done.
> And now her misty curtain
> Kind Autumn softly weaves,
> And spreads a wondrous carpet
> Of gold and silver leaves.

I've learnt many things since – but I'm glad I haven't lost that little song.

*Wednesday 30 October*

To think deeply, to pray and read and listen to music, to revel in a profoundly sensual awareness of the creation – and yet not be bound to it – is to find fullness of life, and to experience a sensitive awareness of the richness and wonder of existence. (So many, today, are content with superficiality – with husks and shells.) But there seems a price to pay, and it takes the form of a special kind of loneliness. Those who live deeply long to communicate in depth.

*Thursday 31 October*

This was my rest day, and a driver's son took me to Breydon – a large expanse of tidal water near Great Yarmouth. John is a keen ornithologist, and together we listed forty-four species: lapwing, starling, skylark, blackbird, cormorant, house-sparrow, common snipe, blue tit, meadow-pipit, fieldfare, pied wagtail, chaffinch, redwing, black-headed gull, rook, greenfinch, heron, rock-pipit, mute swan, reed-bunting, goldfinch, wren, yellow hammer, kingfisher, great black-backed gull, redshank, common gull, barn owl, kestrel, goldeneye, great crested grebe, hedge-sparrow, dunlin, sheld-duck, oyster-catcher, grey plover, black-tailed godwit, herring gull, curlew, moorhen, mallard, pheasant, coot, robin. To be away from the city all day; to see only two other people; to be surrounded by water, marsh, and sky, was soothing and reassuring. I felt part of me was being healed, and I did not want to come away.

Festal evensong: the first evensong of All Saints'. This is one of my favourite festivals, but tonight's was the only service my shifts will permit me to attend. To my dismay I cannot get to the services on either All Saints' Day or All Souls' Day.

*Young men and maidens, old men and children, praise the Name of the Lord: for his Name only is excellent, and his praise above heaven and earth.*

*He shall exalt the horn of his people; all his saints shall praise him: even the children of Israel, even the people that serveth him.*

This evening I attended an induction service at one of the city churches.

*Friday 1 November*

All Saints' Day. The most famous saints have their own days of commemoration; today the church gives thanks also for those whose names often are remembered by God alone. The humanity of the saints should be our inspiration. Though many were weak-willed, or short-tempered, or full of spiritual failings, in each some aspect of Christian discipleship shone with unusual brilliance: courage, or love, or perseverance, or patience, or faith.

A good discussion developed with some youngsters in the pub. Their language may be crude, but their questions are real.

*Saturday 2 November*

All Souls' Day. Today the church commemorates all who have died in faith. While the souls have not shown the qualities so brilliantly displayed by the saints they, too, beckon towards another realm, where growth and fulfilment become possible for all.

On the edge of the city, from my cab I saw a kestrel rise from a grassy bank and fly alongside the moving bus at a distance of only ten yards. I was very excited.

Among my eccentricities must be listed the fact that I sleep in a four-poster bed (made by a driver a few years ago, to my specifications). Bed is not simply the end of the day. It is, in itself, one of the events and pleasures of the day. Time and again I have found that the moment my head touches the pillow I recall some of the details and the feeling of the previous night's dream. I used to think that time spent asleep was time wasted; shifts and alarm clocks have made me see things differently.

*Sunday 3 November*

I baptized the infant son of a bus conductor whose wedding I took about two years ago.

Psalm 116 (not an evensong psalm) was sung this afternoon, and I was moved:

*What reward shall I give unto the Lord: for all the benefits that he hath done unto me?*

In the twilight, a tawny owl was hooting in the ash tree behind our house. Another could be heard faintly, answering in the distance. Always I have found this a mysterious, captivating sound.

*Monday 4 November*

Geoff, a former bus conductor, told me he had used my name for a reference. He filled in the application form as follows:

'*Name:* Rev. J. Burton; *Occupation:* Priest; *Employer:* God.'

Tonight in the pub an irreverent youth said: 'I'm going to buy you a black bra to go with that long black dress I saw you wearing.'

*Tuesday 5 November*

The children had some fireworks, and I was appointed O.C. Bonfire. I guarded it contentedly for two hours, and derived immense satisfaction from the heat and flames.

*Wednesday 6 November*

The Dean's monthly newsletter includes a reference to the psalms: 'I remember as a schoolboy tip-toeing into my father's bedroom. He knew he was dying, I knew he was dying; after we had talked about the garden and school and holidays, with all that careful evasion of things one finds too hard to talk about, I said, "What would you like me to do for you?" He replied, "Read me some of the psalms."

Perhaps in the great experiences of suffering and recovering, of birth and death, when we doubt and when we have faith (and when we have both together, as many of us do), then those old splendid words, asking the questions which matter most and singing the songs of faith, will be pointers on our pilgrimage, now joyful, now very demanding, calling always for honesty and love and faith. "Lord, who shall dwell in thy tabernacle: or who shall rest upon thy holy hill?" "The Lord is my light, and my salvation; whom then shall I fear: the Lord is the strength of my life; of whom then shall I be afraid?" '

*Thursday 7 November*
I drove past a beech-wood; although it was raining, the leaves presented a scene of splendour.

*Friday 8 November*
During our tea-break I overheard Dick, a conductor, telling two good bus stories. A few years ago, his bus was proceeding along a narrow lane. The driver was hurrying, but had to pass a parked lorry loaded with soft-drinks. The bottles stacked on the lorry were slanted at an angle, and as the bus dashed through the gap it brushed against the lorry and removed the top from every bottle of pop along the bottom row!

Not long afterwards the same driver met a heavily-laden hay-cart at the same spot. It was mid-summer, and the bus windows were open. Once more he charged through the gap at good speed, and to the horrified amazement of his conductor filled the interior of the lower deck with hay! The passengers – staring ahead stolidly in true Norfolk fashion – resembled contented cattle bedded down safely for the night.

*My soul is athirst for God, yea, even for the living God: when shall I come to appear before the presence of God?*

*Saturday 9 November*
It is curiously affecting to watch leaves fall on a still day.

*Sunday 10 November*
I am unashamedly sensual. Each day provides an endless succession of insights and experiences which stimulate my spirit and provoke attitudes which can be described only as religious. I will give some examples (though it is a risky and revealing business). I am moved by the *sight* of the countryside bathed in moonlight; by sunlight shining on the trunk of a tree, emphasizing the texture of the bark; by the first brave spring flowers. I like to *feel* the soft pile of velvet material; to handle a piece of carved, polished woodwork; to know the biting air of a frosty morning. I appreciate the *taste* of skate, rare steak, red wine, and Balkan Sobranie. (Religious?!!) I am affected by the *scent* of rain on the earth after a dry spell; by hay (in the evening) which has been cut earlier in the day; by the good, earthy smell of a river; by the breath and sweat of a friend or lover; by honeysuckle; by greasy overalls; by fallen leaves. I am stirred by

the *sound* of thunder; by a robin singing in the coldness of a winter afternoon; by the boy soloist singing 'Hear My Prayer'; by the wind in the trees; by owls.

I revel in these sensations. The creation shouts aloud to me of God. I am driven to the conclusion that there is a proper, Christian sensuality; a reverent sensuality which tantalizes and beckons beyond; a sensuality both voluptuous and pure; an honesty in experience; a sensitivity and discernment. Without killing the mystery, I try to draw the last ounce of sensation from every experience. For to be knowingly and consciously sensual is to be vividly and vibrantly *alive* – alive and awake and alert. In that open, receptive, and vulnerable state we become most human; and most accessible to God.

*Monday 11 November*

My winter holiday commenced today. I went for a long country walk, ignoring the rain but stopping to watch a small flock of ten long-tailed tits. I gathered some conkers for the children, and marvelled at their irresistibility: neatly-rounded, shiny and smooth, handsomely-coloured.

*Tuesday 12 November*

The main task during the winter holiday is tidying the garden; today I made a start.

*O come hither, and behold the works of God: how wonderful he is in his doing toward the children of men.*

God seems to get all the credit and none of the blame.

*Wednesday 13 November*

One disagreeable incident can ruin a whole day. People can be hateful and comtemtpible.

*Thy rebuke hath broken my heart; I am full of heaviness: I looked for some to have pity on me, but there was no man, neither found I any to comfort me.*

*They gave me gall to eat: and when I was thirsty they gave me vinegar to drink.*

*Thursday 14 November*

A violent storm broke at mid-day; it grew so dark I couldn't see to continue working in the garden.

*Then thought I to understand this: but it was too hard for me, Until I went into the sanctuary of God: then understood I the end of these men.* 

I am enjoying my holiday and am glad, for a while, to leave the crowd. But I miss my friends – and I miss my cab! This is an immense paradox, but my cab is like a cloister. Although it is the focal point of my identification with the world, it is – at one and the same time – the place where I sit in solitude for hours, and where all kinds of thoughts flash through my mind.

I am so rich that I feel ashamed.

*Friday 15 November*

The long and immensely powerful seventy-eighth psalm was sung at evensong:

*So man did eat angels' food.*

Simon, the irreverent youth, said: 'I'm sorry to hear about your back trouble, vicar. That *is* why you wear the white support round your neck, isn't it?'

*Saturday 16 November*

I've pruned the roses severely. One bud on a discarded branch was opening, so we brought it into the house and in the warmth it has unfolded. It's a Fragrant Cloud – slightly paler than the earlier blooms, but with a scent that confirms my blatant sensuality. For us, this is literally the last rose of summer, and it has given more pleasure than all the magnificent blooms of June and July.

*Sunday 17 November*

I finished *Go Tell It On The Mountain* by James Baldwin, and immediately started another of his books.

This record is not a detailed diary: I'm not concerned to chronicle everything I do – each meeting, service, conversation, and engagement. I was at three services today, preaching twice: but those are not matters of interest. I want to note the amusing and significant events; and my thoughts and reactions.

*Monday 18 November*

As it rained hard all day, I declared the year's gardening closed, and returned from the herbaceous border to my desk and typewriter.

*Take heed, ye unwise among the people: O ye fools, when will ye understand? He that planted the ear, shall he not hear: or he that made the eye, shall he not see?*

*Tuesday 19 November*

*O magnify the Lord our God; and fall down before his footstool, for he is holy.*

The second book by James Baldwin was *Giovanni's Room*, which I found compelling and upsetting:

'There are so many ways of being despicable it quite makes one's head spin. But the way to be really despicable is to be contemptuous of other people's pain. You ought to have some apprehension that the man you see before you was once even younger than you are now and arrived at his present wretchedness by imperceptible degrees.'

'Love him and let him love you. Do you think anything else under heaven really matters?'[1]

*Wednesday 20 November*

The feast of St Edmund, king and martyr, patron of East Anglia.

The Union sent one of the brothers to discuss a matter with me (although I have been out of office for nearly a year). I was glad to be of assistance.

*O Lord, how manifold are thy works: in wisdom hast thou made them all; the earth is full of thy riches.*

*Thursday 21 November*

I enjoyed thoroughly a cathedral event entitled 'Language, Light, and Liturgy – From Advent to All Saints'. My favourite items were:

Palestrina, 'Dum complerentur Dies Pentecostes'
S. S. Wesley, 'Cast me not away'
C. V. Stanford, 'Coelos ascendit hodie'
Arthur Wills, 'The Praises of the Trinity'
Olivier Messiaen, 'Les Mages' (from *La Nativité du Seigneur*)

Birmingham bomb outrage.

*Friday 22 November*

*But deal thou with me, O Lord God, according unto thy Name: for sweet is thy mercy.*

An excellent discussion developed in the pub tonight, with several people joining in.

[1] James Baldwin, *Giovanni's Room*, Michael Joseph 1957, pp. 81f., 83. Reprinted by permission of A. D. Peters & Co. Ltd.

*Saturday 23 November*

The feast of St Clement.

The bus I drove this morning must have just come off the pits and. my hands, when I glanced at them, were covered in oil. My immediate reaction was one of annoyance, but when I looked again I was intrigued. The oil had highlighted every line and print; I felt that I was seeing my hands for the first time, and I was astonished that dirty oil should reveal such intricacy and beauty.

I never cease to wonder what it is that draws people into relationship. Perhaps it is solely a chemical process, the workings of which are not yet clear to us. Sometimes, I think the attraction arises from similarity of temperament and interest; at other times it seems based upon contrast! Usually, however, the process works at a deeper and more subtle level. Why we 'click' with certain people – and by 'click' I think I mean fall a little in love – is a mystery before which I marvel daily. For me, this is the stark wonder of creature man: that one small quantity of dust and earth should experience an attraction, an affinity, a desire, a connection with another small quantity of similar material. You may fill two buckets with mud, but – so far as we are aware – one load will not fall in love or friendship with the other though you wait till the wind blows away both as dust. So while chemical processes may be involved, I am interested more in the creative energy which fashions and holds the mud into the shape of a man, and animates him for a brief period with the gift of life.

Chemistry cannot destroy the mystery of being and loving; it describes 'how' rather than 'why'. I refuse utterly to consider myself the helpless slave of my own chemistry; that may determine when I die, but that alone shall not decide the way I live. I will accept fully a 'chemical' explanation of other people's bad behaviour, but I will never make it a personal excuse.

It is good to be close to a number of people (although the most precious relationships will be few indeed). Our personalities have countless facets and immeasurable depths, and each relationship plays upon a different part of our make-up. Each person draws from us something new and distinctive because our response is dependent partly upon their unique stimulus. The more aspects of our personality which find expression in vital relationships the richer we become.

Nº 4498

*Sunday 24 November*

At evensong I heard a haunting and unusual anthem: 'Jehovah quam multi sunt hostes' – a setting of psalm 3 by Purcell.

*Monday 25 November*

Late shifts are not very attractive in winter. Their one advantage is that they give me almost a whole day to use as I choose.

*Tuesday 26 November*

I've hit (rather quickly) another of those periods when nothing goes right. One might as well give up. The harder you try, the worse it gets. I need Breydon again, badly.

*Wednesday 27 November*

One of the most important concepts in modern thinking about the mission of the church is the notion of Christian 'presence'. This means more than witnessing because you happen to be present; it means entering a situation deliberately, becoming part of the situation, and watching with Christ. It is not, alas, guaranteed to increase congregations, but it produces endless opportunities of contact-at-depth with those who find belief difficult. For that reason, providing a Christian presence seems to me one of the comparatively few forms of evangelism which still makes sense in this astonishing age. If we will not give ourselves to the world, in the flesh, our continued and rapid retrenchment is inevitable. But ministers and laymen alike can initiate schemes of presence, by entering 'centres of influence' in the community (from council to pub) – and by staying there. This approach is in closest harmony with the great festival for which we are about to prepare.

*Thursday 28 November*

Roy and I had one of our frequent sessions in praise of steam, and mourned that the glory of the Lord had departed. My favourite steam railway locomotives were the streamlined A4s of the old LNER which, with many other famous classes, were shouts of creative triumph, expressions of cosmic magnificence! A3s and A4s; Schools and West Countrys; Jubilees and Royal Scots; Kings, Castles, and Halls – these fiery giants affected every nerve and sense: the sight of a double-headed express thundering up an incline; the roars and shrieks and whistles; the taste and smell of smoke and

A4 Pacific 'Sir Nigel Gresley' passing through York station

 steam; the thrill of touching polished metal! Steam locomotives were a sublime demonstration of man's partnership with the creation. The skill of designers, and the beauty of line they produced; the technical ability of engineers and builders; the courage and confidence and sure-touch of drivers; the rippling muscles and the sweat of firemen; the combination of fire and water and coal and sparks and speed – it was drama and spectacle and poetry rolled into one.

Here was the embodiment of energy and power. Here was man confronting the elements. Here was the primaeval conflict between man and his environment. Here was the dirt and the glory of human existence; inheritance and endeavour; earth and heaven. In these intuitive impressions lay the magic of steam. Perhaps modern children draw similar nourishment from pictures of space-ships – though I doubt it. Steam locomotives were more than pieces of machinery; it is only a small exaggeration to say they lived. I saw stripped A4s on a scrap-line at Norwich. The sight was grotesque and vile.

*Friday 29 November*

In the pub I remarked that I was trying to think of a subject for my next sermon. A teenage girl suggested immediately: 'The sinfulness of man, and how nice it is.' I think she knows more about sex than she does about sin – and confuses the two.

*Saturday 30 November*

I attended a commendable production of *Hamlet*. Of all the lines and phrases from the tragedy which have become integral parts of the English language, I treasure most the advice given by Polonius to the departing Laertes:

> This above all: to thine own self be true,
> And it must follow, as the night the day,
> Thou canst not then be false to any man.

*Sunday 1 December*

At the cathedral this evening, 'A Procession with Carols' to celebrate the first Sunday in Advent was dramatic and richly satisfying: darkness and light, colour and symbol, music and movement combined to produce a powerful atmosphere of expectancy and penitence and celebration. Advent hymns and responses were interspersed with carols sung by the choir, of which my favourites were 'Gabriel's

Message', 'There is no rose of such virtue', and 'The Lord at first did Adam make'. 

*Monday 2 December*
Roy, who has been good company, seems tired of conducting and is thinking of leaving, so today I started working with another conductor whose driver transferred recently to one-man operation. Tony is twenty-two and plays football and records. I am certain we shall form a crack crew!

*The words of the Lord are pure words: even as the silver, which from the earth is tried, and purified seven times in the fire.*

*Tuesday 3 December*
One week ago I was gloomy and miserable; this week I am ready to face anything! How fickle I am! I sit in the cab singing 'All the way my saviour leads me; what have I to ask beside?' – but when he leads me through the valley I panic and squeal. I do not deserve all I have been given.

*Wednesday 4 December*
Recently, large flocks of waxwings have been reported in East Anglia, and I kept a special look-out on a country run this morning, but without success. The only waxwing I have ever seen was observed from the cab of my bus two years ago. A brownish-pink coloured bird flew across the road at Costessey. For a split-second I could not identify it, until I saw a bar of brilliant yellow at the tip of its tail: then I knew it was a waxwing, and was overjoyed.

*Thursday 5 December*
I saw a brilliant shooting-star from the bus station yard at 5.45 this morning.

*The Lord shall give strength unto his people: the Lord shall give his people the blessing of peace.*

*Friday 6 December*
The Christmas roses in the garden look very beautiful.

*Saturday 7 December*
After our shift, Tony and I went to the football match. The second half was terrible.

A girl in the pub drew a hurried self-portrait on a scrap of paper somebody produced. I was very impressed, and when everyone else had forgotten it, I salvaged it carefully from a pool of spilled beer. 

*Sunday 8 December*

I conducted evening worship at the church I attended as a teenager, which – after all – is not so *very* long ago! Then, there would have been over forty in the congregation, including a good crowd of youngsters: tonight, there were sixteen, and the service was held in the schoolroom to save heating the large church.

Afterwards, I indulged in an orgy of nostalgia. I stood outside the terraced house and looked up at the bedroom where I was born. I walked slowly through the alley where we played football all the year round – ('Please can we have our ball back?') – together with other seasonal pastimes which appeared in annual rotation: five-stones, cigarette-cards, conkers, and many others. I saw the shed where I received a fairly thorough grounding in the basic facts of life, for which always I have been grateful. It came as a shock, looking back, to realize that – once initiated – I sinned more than I was sinned against, and often set out deliberately to seduce my instructor when he was engaged, perfectly contentedly, on a piece of woodwork or some other enterprise. (I *never* found out why they painted it with turps one day, though.)

The dug-out where I gave my impetigo to the boy next door (who was older, and to whom I was devoted) as the war neared its end has long been filled-in; the magnificent double-white lilac I remember so clearly has been cut down; the pig-bin in the corner of a yard (where women deposited their peelings and swill, and which attracted wasps by the multitude in summer) is no longer in position: but my initials are still carved on the wall where they have been for twenty-five years, and I paused to gaze at them. I strolled up the hill down which we sped on sledges in winter and – more dangerously – on soap-box trolleys in summer; passed the bowling-green where occasionally I wiped bowls; and came to the home of some old friends who have known me since those days – indeed, who watched my mother call for *her* school-friend at the house opposite, several years prior to my arrival!

Whatever does it mean – these memories, this ever-accelerating experience we call life? I like returning to these streets. They take me back, swiftly and powerfully, to – to what? Almost, to a different

'A crack crew.'

me – bright, eager, innocent. I say *almost*. Sometimes, I feel I have been on a long, unavoidable, essential journey (during which I was robbed and rewarded), only to return from whence I came. Now, at thirty-five, I begin to recognize myself, and can identify with the fair-haired boy aged between five and ten who ran about these streets kicking tennis-balls and bowling hoops. At thirty-five I am closer to that boy than I was at fifteen plus, when many conflicts raged and guilt had a field-day, aided and abetted by holy church; closer, even, than at twenty-five, when I was worried about the meaning of obedience to the church, and perturbed by the mysterious complexity of human nature. That has passed, as so much water under the bridge. And I look at those initials gratefully, anxious to secure my identity, anxious for confirmation that it really was me, and making the ironic discovery – in the calm after the storm – that I was not far away, as a small boy, from that for which most of us proceed to spend the rest of our lives searching. And neither were the other boys and girls.

There is a catholicity about childhood which is filched from us – and for many it is lost for ever. Sex experiments in the air-raid shelters (which then stood obligingly at nearly every street-corner) were part of the same experience, the same world, the same daily existence, as the cry of the brown owl hooting in the wooded cemetery where we loved to play (and where we were chased by old Palmer, the keeper). School and football; the sun setting behind the cathedral; days of thick fog; the horse-and-cart bolting down the hill; my contempt for the irrelevancy of Sunday School, and my near reverence for a 'blackies' nest with four eggs; beech-nuts; old buses painted in grey wartime camouflage; handsome green and orange acorns from the turkey oak; steam-rollers; the Yanks, ('Got any gum, chum?'); listening to the band in the bandstand on the heath – all these were woven together in an exciting tapestry which was ever new and fresh and inviting. There was an underlying unity, and a daily, spontaneous, innocent celebration of the sheer wonder and goodness of the creation.

I never lost it completely – but it was a near thing. Perhaps 'growing-up' inevitably involves loss as well as gain, shrinkage as well as growth. I remember the first girl I hung around specially to see: the first girl who ever registered as being more than just 'a girl'. She showed no interest in me (and went eventually to Australia!), but she was a significant straw in the wind of adolescent change.

Not long after came an evangelical religious conversion, and with it a new vocabulary and the concept of sin. Looking back (and only with gratitude, not regrets), I feel that the experience which was induced and the religious tradition of evangelical Christianity into which I was drawn were set slightly at half-cock. It seems to me at least possible that the colour, light, symbol, ritual, and drama of catholic Christianity might have built more naturally upon the exuberant foundations of boyhood. But that was not to be, and I bear thankfulness – not resentment – towards those who drew aside the curtain and allowed me to glimpse the mystery of the divine love. Given that secret, the possibilities become endless; and no shortcomings in the ecclesiastical 'system' can prevent those who have recognized Jesus as the word made flesh from becoming gradually aware of the word throbbing through creation. They have only to be true to the light that is in them, not mimicking the opinions of others, but humbly and fearlessly pursuing truth, and accepting truth; particularly the truth about themselves.

*Monday 9 December*

When, with my wife and children, I was homeless and desperate, a couple in their seventies found an old cottage for us to rent, which they scrubbed and tidied from top to bottom. (This was when I left the security of the manse and first embarked on a 'worker-priest' ministry.) For the seven months we lived there, they were our neighbours and cared for us like parents. I do not forget such kindness. It was beyond description; it was so sweet and good that it made heavy burdens light, and because it was offered freely and naturally and quietly and unconditionally it placed me eternally and gladly in their debt.

I buried Herbert in May, and controlled my voice only with difficulty – and then not with complete success. 'That old man really loved you,' his wife told me, and my eyes burned hot with tears. He was eighty-one, and his death deepened my loneliness. I made a special journey to visit Edith today. She has missed him terribly. They would have been married sixty years this month. Each night, in bed, she sings the funeral hymns: 'Peace, Perfect Peace', and 'For ever with the Lord!'

Cheered and saddened by my visit, I was touched to receive seasonal greetings from friends to whom once I ministered: 'As we draw near to worship at the manger, we remember you with love and gratitude.' Those generous words comforted me. Thus do we minister, and are ministered unto. 

At sunset there was a gorgeous orange afterglow.

*Tuesday 10 December*

*And I said, O that I had wings like a dove: for then would I flee away, and be at rest.*

A bitterly cold afternoon, with a predominantly yellow afterglow.

I attended a meeting of the Industrial Commission of the local council of churches. I am not (as many insist on believing) an industrial chaplain, but I respect their work. They enter what is, for them, an alien environment, and try to establish contact with persons of influence on both sides of industry. They attempt to promote and increase mutual trust and reconciliation; they raise value-judgments concerning the nature of man and the meaning of work; they pursue the pastoral opportunities which present themselves. It is genuine and costly mission.

My own concerns are more narrowly 'religious' – in the widest, most catholic sense! I want simply to live and work in the world, as a man and as a believer; I want to provide a Christian presence, a centre of compassion and acceptance – and see what happens!

A wild-life film on television late tonight featured the lammergeier, and I watched this vulture (whose wing-span measures nine feet) with astonishment, captivated by the grace and beauty of its flight.

*Wednesday 11 December*

It snowed for just under an hour this morning – large flakes, now falling quietly, now driven madly before the wind.

This afternoon I noticed that where the gulls were following the plough a few weeks ago the green winter barley is growing.

*They go to and fro in the evening: they grin like a dog, and run about through the city.*

*Thursday 12 December*

This month's book is *Portrait of a Lady* by Henry James.

*Friday 13 December*

Listening to people, and watching, and thinking, I wonder occasionally if sex *does* matter as much as I assume – if it really *is* involved in all our actions and reactions. If you get plenty, it doesn't seem quite so vitally important; but if you are tormented with curiosity, or inflamed with passion, nothing matters more.

Another afterglow of great beauty – salmon-pink and orange.

*Saturday 14 December*

Tony blurted out: 'I hope we don't get caught in a jaffic tram.'

Truly, there is something frightening about love, about emotional enslavement to another. It is sweet beyond words, but it is so helpless! Unless and until the experience becomes mutual, and an emotional circuit is established, love is an immense drain on any person's spiritual resources.

*Sunday 15 December*

St Clement's church possesses a silver Elizabethan chalice of great beauty which – in its way – is as perfect an example of craftsmanship as an A4 locomotive. It has a bell-shaped cup, and is fitted with a matching paten/cover. The heel of the paten bears the inscription: 1569 SAYNCT CLEMENTS OF FYBRYG WARD. The chalice is inscribed: THE GYFTE OF SESSELY SVFYLD.

Cicely Suffield was the last prioress of Carrow Abbey, a religious house near the city boundary dedicated to the Blessed Virgin Mary and St John. It housed a prioress and twelve Benedictine nuns. Cicely Suffield had a pension of five pounds per annum assigned to her at the Dissolution, and settled eventually in this parish in a house next to the churchyard, opposite my own. Earlier it had been the city house of the priors of Ixworth, in Suffolk, and parts of it remain. Her burial is recorded in the Parish Register: 'Cicely Suffield was buryed ye 13 of July 1565'. The communion chalice commemorates her bequests to the parish.

A marble slab in the nave of the church has this inscription: 'Here lyeth the bodye of Symond Bullocke Mr of arte & late psone of this parishe who decessed the vi daye of October An. Dni. 1574.' He offered the body and blood of Christ to his people at the altar of this church from this very paten and chalice.

Foulk Roberts, one of the most interesting of the clergy of Norwich past and present, was minister here in the seventeenth century. Having incurred the wrath of the Puritans, he was turned out of his living during the Civil War and forced to live in great poverty until his death. He handled this cup.

In 1705 the Master and Fellows of Gonville and Caius College, Cambridge, became patrons of the church, and during the eighteenth century the living was held by men of academic ability. Norwich was then the third largest city in England. Its prosperity was due largely to the worsted industry, and some of the most prominent manufacturers – commemorated by the mural monuments – resided in this parish. They received the sacrament from this chalice and paten. One Victorian rector was minister here for nearly forty-four years. He held this silver. 

These beautiful, antique pieces symbolize the eternal Christ who feeds and upholds and renews his people in every generation. They provide a solid, visible link with those who have gone before, reminding us that the church in heaven and earth is one, and the veil between narrow and insubstantial. I think often of those who have sipped wine from this very cup; their world seemed as solid and real to them as ours appears now to us. But, inevitably, we shall join them; others will kneel where now we kneel: and the pageant will continue.

*Monday 16 December*

Have you ever been so joyful in the presence of another person that you feel sure the whole world must be aware of your gladness? The sensitive and imaginative probably *are* aware. Love is gaiety, and gaiety irrepressible. But we have become strangers to love, afraid of love; and therefore 'the whole world' doesn't always recognize love when it sees it. Which – if it is a relief – is rather a pity; for love enriches those it touches and those who see through its light disguise. And the universe is pregnant with love. The spark of warmth can ignite spontaneously at any instant, between any persons.

*Tuesday 17 December*

One terminus we visit regularly is situated at a hospital, and a row of old men are often to be found seated on a bench beside the bus stop. One, in particular, is there usually from early morning until late in the evening, summer and winter. The arrival of a bus is an important occasion, for quickly he checks both decks for short-ends; the remainder of the day is spent in two ways. He thumbs endlessly through magazines and periodicals, pulling at each page; and he draws. Everyone knows his drawings; they are placed on the wall for all to see – and always they are the same. Fred draws two things only – pheasants and dove-cotes, day after day after day. At one time I felt I would go crazy if I saw those drawings any more: pheasants and dove-cotes, pheasants and dove-cotes – it seemed a maddening daily refrain. But I've changed, and now I look forward to seeing them. The symbolism they express eludes me – yet I fancy I could base a meditation upon them concerning the beauty of the earth, the goodness of food, English country gardens, church choirs, peace and reconciliation, 'Also the Holy Ghost: the Comforter'! All these are themes dear to me.

*Wednesday 18 December*
I watched the dawn while driving on a country route. We left the city with headlights on, but by the time we reached our destination a new day had broken, bright and clear.

Tony and I devised a new terminus pastime, testing each other on the names of the Football League clubs' grounds. He was surprised that I knew so many.

A delicate-purple sunset.

*The Lord is King, and hath put on glorious apparel: the Lord hath put on his apparel, and girded himself with strength.*

*Thursday 19 December*
Evensong included one of my favourite anthems – 'Call to Remembrance, O Lord', by Richard Farrant. I was deeply moved and could have wept during the psalms, particularly the last (psalm 101, Webb in D):

*My song shall be of mercy and judgement: unto thee, O Lord, will I sing.*
*O let me have understanding: in the way of godliness.*
*When wilt thou come unto me: I will walk in my house with a perfect heart.*
*I will take no wicked thing in hand; I hate the sins of unfaithfulness: there shall no such cleave unto me.*

If it were only so.

*Whoso leadeth a godly life: he shall be my servant.*

I felt restless this evening. I crossed the road and went into St Clement's, and filled it thick with incense. There I remained, and the darkness and stillness healed me.

*Friday 20 December*
I intended to visit the cathedral shop; Tony was with me. At the

cathedral door (wanting always to be fair about these things), I said to him, 'You can either wait here, or come in.' He said he would go in, and as we made to open the door the Dean came out. My conductor seemed proud to have met the Dean of Norwich; I hope that for his part, he was sensible of the privilege of having met the best bus conductor in the city!

Inside the great building – decorated for Christmas – Tony looked round and said, 'Is this for everyone?' I wasn't sure exactly what he meant: 'Can anyone walk round here at any time?' 'Can anyone come to the services here?' But I didn't stop to ask – I answered immediately and emphatically, 'Yes, of course.' It was a good question.

I returned for a carol service this evening. Strangely, it lacked (for me) the impact of the Advent carol service; but many of my favourites were included – in particular 'The Three Kings', by Cornelius.

*Saturday 21 December*

I went to the football match with Tony and my son, Trevor. Norwich City went ahead after seventeen minutes with a goal scored direct from a corner, but were unable to produce the finishing which would have increased their lead. Then disaster struck: Bristol City equalized in the forty-first minute, and before our dismay had subsided, went ahead in the forty-second minute – and it was half-time. We were deep in gloom. The start of the second half was painful to watch, and we began to wish we had stayed at home. Then it happened! In the sixty-fifth minute Phil Boyer snatched the equalizer. Our celebrations were still in progress when, in the sixty-sixth minute, he scored again to put Norwich back in the lead. We went wild with excitement, and that was the result: a 3–2 victory.

A damp and mild autumn has ended.

*Sunday 22 December*

Henri Perrin, French Jesuit worker-priest:

'Far from dominating us, these godless men are in our hands, for the most part poor creatures who ask for light and friendship. Yes, of course, they won't be coming to Mass next Sunday, and it's much better that they shouldn't. But they need a Christian near them, someone who is attractive and doesn't think like everyone else, who behaves in a way that it is a witness to the existence of another world where life is happier because people believe in something beyond themselves. I've seen them full of astonishment and admiration when they learned about our prayers, our friendship, and our faith. We may not be much in ourselves, but at least they've met Christians, a thing that doesn't happen every day.'[1]

*Monday 23 December*

Institutions – by reason of their complexity, antiquity, or rigidity – are ever prone to conceal the very realities they exist to embody! The church is no exception, and Christians must be aware that reverence for the church is no substitute for love of Christ. The Christmas story should preserve us from such temptations. The feast of the nativity of our Lord is celebrated in beautiful buildings, with the noblest expressions of devotion that man can devise, and the loftiest worship to which his spirit can aspire: glorious music, great congregations, processions and carols, impressive colour, time-honoured ritual. It is right and proper. We are celebrating the birth of God in human form; the intermingling of human and divine.

But the words we hear speak of poverty, homelessness, lack of privilege. The story is about a child born in squalor, who grew up to work at a manual trade. There was no reason why God should not have been born in a palace. Had the planning been in our hands, we would have arranged matters in more seemly fashion. But God is unseemly; 'He . . . hath exalted the humble and meek.' (Let us hope the words do not choke us.) God's ways are not our ways; his standards of judgment are not the criteria we employ. Let us celebrate his coming, and offer worship and service in worthiest adoration; but let us be glad that God has given no monopoly of insight and faithfulness to the wealthy, the educated, and the respectable. That is not his way. Those low in the social scale, those who lack academic brilliance, those whose speech is rough – these may conceivably be greater in the kingdom of God. That is the reality. 'Blessed are the pure in heart.' But born in a stable! It was hardly decent.

*Tuesday 24 December*

Tony and I looked in at evensong for three minutes during our

[1] Henri Perrin, *Priest and Worker: An Autobiography*, Macmillan 1965, p. 49.

break. At the close of the shift we went to a pub near the garage which was packed with busmen: it was rather like a Christmas edition of a television serial – everyone seemed to be there. We had a few pints, and then I went home; I was to preach at midnight mass. 

That fact had been much on my mind over recent days, and I had not been able to work out a sermon which felt 'right'. I was strongly tempted to rehash some old material, but I didn't want to do so unless all else failed. That was the position when I went to work early this afternoon. Then I began to notice people . . . and incidents . . . and from my cab I tried to relate these to the child and to this holy night. Soon I was glad and filled with thankfulness. I had been given a word to speak: not a dry old sermon, warmed-up; but a message only hours old, wrung out of the events of the afternoon. At each terminus, while Tony watched with amused interest, I struggled to put my still-vague thoughts into order and jot down one hundred and fifty words of notes. I felt I was taking a risk in trusting for the right words to come, but my mind was made up.

I enjoy the Christmas midnight mass. It is one of those special 'occasions' to which usually I can respond. But never before had I preached after four pints of beer. I was aware of the danger. I felt mildly guilty – get the pun? – but not much. The sermon was an immediate product of my way of life. True, my notes were completed before the beer was drunk, and I *could* have allowed Tony to join the others in the pub on his own, without his driver. But that would have been cheating, and you can't cheat like that in the pattern of existence I have adopted. Tonight's sermon came out of a way of life of which, this evening, beer was an integral part. No beer, no sermon. No rough-and-tumbled mixing in the world and getting dirty, no word from the manger. (The fourth pint was not with the busmen – it was in my parish local where I felt obliged to call, extending Christmas greetings and being kissed. Albeit very pleasant, it was – as I explained to my wife – a duty!)

I know I am very wicked, yet I am not sure always exactly in what my wickedness consists. (Sometimes, I am very sure.) I did not, of course, fall out of the pulpit, and the sermon proved the most effective piece of oratory I have produced since my strike-call at the branch meeting a year ago. The entire service was an act of celebration and gladness, and a spirit of joy and love filled the church.

Sermon outline: 

I like a religious argument, with plenty of cut-and-thrust, at any time – except tonight. Except on Christmas Eve. My conductor said to me tonight: 'Virgin? She couldn't have been.' But I would not discuss it. For this is a night of magic; a time of expectation, and excitement, and worship. This is the most special of all nights.

I have been trying to relate the people and events I've seen today with the great event we celebrate tonight.

Twelve glimpses:

1. Visited an old man in his eighties who has just had a serious heart-attack. His dear wife is so anxious, and so cheerful.

2. Noticed a young, engaged couple I know, completing their Christmas shopping. (The girl has a beautiful, gipsy face – would make a splendid Mary in a nativity play.)

3. Standing in the crowded street at the start of my shift, waiting for the bus to arrive, many people whom I knew passed. All were cheerful; all exchanged greetings.

What meaning has the child – for these?

4. A young conductor caught our bus and alighted at the hospital. He was visiting his baby son, very ill.

5. A well-known local vagrant carrying all his worldly possessions in six carrier-bags.

6. In the three minutes it took to leave the main road, reach the terminus, and return to the main road again, a new car had crashed into a set of traffic-lights, and looked a definite write-off.

Just pictures – not explanations or discussions.

What meaning has the child – for these?

7. A choirboy late for evensong.

8. Two young bloods (who buy me a drink sometimes), off to the fair dressed to kill. I blow the horn to attract their attention, and they wave and shout exuberantly as the bus passes.

9. An old man who lives in a hostel, shuffling along . . .

What meaning has the child – for these?

10. A police-car parked outside a house where the blinds are drawn. Two policemen are talking on the step with a man holding

 a bag, who looks like a doctor.

11. A school with the decorations still up, but with all the desks empty, and the chairs neatly stacked. (Those children should just about be asleep by now!)

12. A house where the past year has brought separation and impending divorce. There is a decoration in the window, but inside the house is a deathly silence. The children have gone with her.

It was not into a make-believe world of robins, tinsel, and reindeer
But
Into a world where men and women suffer and grow old, fall in love, work together, become friends, grieve for their children, wander as vagrants, make mistakes, find themselves in a hurry, are happy-go-lucky, feel unloved, worry, die alone, watch children playing, break each other's hearts –
a baby was born.

Tony in the cathedral – 'Is this for everyone?' – 'Yes, of course.'
This child – This Christmas 'thing' – These carols . . .
Is *this* for everyone? Yes, of course.
This baby brought a new dimension to human experience.
By being born in a stable and not a palace; by being the son of a peasant girl rather than a princess; by his acts of mercy and compassion; by his mingling easily with all types of people; by his teaching that the greatest and most truly blessed are those who serve and humbly reckon others more important than themselves; by his weeping over the city; by his death and by his resurrection, this child cast a new light on what it means to be a human being . . .

On this wonderful night old wrongs and grievances fall away. We see how few of them were ever really important. It's Christmas Eve, and no one should be excluded.
Tonight, I do not argue. Tonight, I do not contend.
Tonight, I ponder.
Tonight, I adore.

*Wednesday 25 December*
Lord Jesus Christ,
Child of Mary,
Be incarnate in this flesh.
May that mind be in me
Which was in Christ Jesus my Lord.

One of the Christmas presents which brought me particular pleasure was a record of Matthew Locke's 'Music for His Majesty's Sackbutts and Cornets'. This was performed during the progress of King Charles II from the Tower of London through the City to Whitehall on 22 April 1661 – the day before his coronation. This suite has a haunting air which stirs and unsettles me.

By late this evening the magic was gone – not the joy nor the gladness, but the wonder of Christmas Eve. The gift had been given. It was like an ordinary, wet, winter's night – which symbolized for me, again, the harsh realities of the world into which the child was born.

*Thursday 26 December*

The feast of St Stephen.

We take for granted the happiness of family life, just as we accept the gift of good health – yet both are precious beyond price. Their true worth is understood best by those to whom they have been denied. Christmas is a reminder of the importance and centrality of the family.

*Friday 27 December*

Dan Billany and David Dowie in *The Cage*, quoted by Monica Furlong in *Travelling In* – another Christmas gift I have appreciated greatly:

'I begin to think, after a year in prison, that the only thing that really matters on earth is that a man should escape from his isolation. That he should be able to drop *all* screens and defences. That people should not be afraid of each other. That human beings should cherish the human life in each other, and love all things human. That is the lesson I get out of prison. Love one another. You can't just start doing it, as the bogus Christians think, by repeating the words aloud; the word deputises much too readily for the fact. You have to do precisely what Christ said – throw away all your defences . . . and make yourself utterly vulnerable, as Christ was to Judas and Pilate. You have to expose your soul, make the great gesture of trust; you have to cast *all* your bread upon the waters. To be strong, admit your weakness; to be safe, accept all danger. To lose all fear, take off your armour and throw away your sword . . .'[1]

[1] Dan Billany and David Dowie, *The Cage*, Longmans 1949. *Travelling In* is published by Hodder & Stoughton, 1971; paperback ed. 1973.

*Saturday 28 December*
Some thoughts in the cab:

You cannot give yourself to people conditionally. You cannot say (in effect) 'I will love you until 4.15: after that you're on your own.'

I have no great yearning to travel: but I *would* like to see Venice.

Some people confess their love and expect it, thereafter, to be assumed; others like to be told again and again. Why should they not be told? The sun is new every morning.

*Sunday 29 December*
The exceptionally mild weather, with no severe ground frosts, has left many gardens full of spring and summer flowers: carnations, polyanthus, pansies, chrysanthemums, and – where they have not been cut back – masses of roses. In our small garden, the Christmas roses and jasmine have been joined by aconites and one narcissus.

*Monday 30 December*
As I walked to work, the full moon had moved into the western sky and begun to pale. The day was born in a blaze of fiery red which burned low in the east while the rest of the sky remained strangely dark. The bare trees were silhouetted starkly against the fire until at length the sky lighted into the most delicate blue, and a slight frost glistened on the car roofs.

*Tuesday 31 December*
There is no rational reason why New Year's Eve should be more solemn an occasion than any other night of the year, nor more sobering than a birthday or wedding anniversary – and brave souls find consolation in the fact. For me, however, New Year's Eve is the antithesis of Christmas Eve: the hope and the magic are replaced by a morose brooding. The clock turns prosecuting counsel and accuses me of sin and futility and failure. Accordingly, I read Bernard Levin's article in *The Times* today with sympathy, relieved that I was not alone and grateful for the existence of another inadequate person:

'. . . I have tried facing the Problem of New Year's Eve in every possible way. I have seen the New Year in at large parties and at small parties; I have spent it *à deux*, sometimes at home and sometimes out; I have spent it alone by my own hearth and alone elsewhere; I have worn a funny hat; I have clasped hands and sung

Auld Lang Syne; I have been to the Watch-night Service at St Paul's; I have been among the crowd in Piccadilly Circus; I have burst into tears; I have switched the phone off and gone to bed before midnight and ignored the whole damned thing; and as far as I can recall I have, almost without exception, felt an overwhelming urge, as the clock struck, to go and hang myself.

For a melancholic of Slav descent, which is what I am, New Year's Eve might have been especially designed to lead to that dread step; we who have an uneasy sense of the futility of life at the best of times have it still more intensely at the moment when the universe pauses, takes a deep breath, and starts again. In the pause, the non-existent instant between year and year, I experience what the drowning man is said to go through, my whole past life being summoned before me as if on some diabolical screen, flickering with the flames of hell. It was Thurber who said that we can all face the great tragedies of our lives, the failed marriages and lost jobs and irreparable quarrels, but it is the tiny incidents, the trivial embarrassments, the word spoken in haste and never to be taken back, it is these things, which everybody else has long since forgotten, "that cause us to pull the bedclothes up over our heads at three o'clock in the morning and *scream*"; for me, all those three o'clocks in the morning come together, in the shape of bats and vultures and shapeless shadows, at midnight on New Year's Eve.'[1]

The year died in a spectacular sunset of reds, pinks, purples, and oranges. In the event, the evening was the best for which I could have hoped. Michael, one of my former conductors (now a driver), called with his wife and small son. They were waiting for the taxi to take them home when the clock struck. Caught off-guard, my spirit experienced an involuntary spasm, and I began to panic – then it was over. But I was left empty and restless, and filled with a mood of vague longing which probably will take a day or two to evaporate.

*Wednesday 1 January 1975*

Christianity means different things to different people; to me, when all the views and interpretations have been shared, Christianity is ultimately about one thing: it is about entering into a mystical relationship of love with Jesus.

Love is not easy to describe or express with scientific accuracy! Love finds its most natural expression in poetry and song – yet

[1] Reproduced from *The Times* by permission.

because of that we do not dismiss the notion of being in love as unreal or fanciful. In the same way, it is not easy to attempt a detailed outline of the love-life of the soul with Jesus; love cannot be categorized neatly into formulas, and the love of the creature for its creator and saviour must ever defy analysis. Those without sympathy for the Christian faith will describe this relationship with Jesus in critical terms: imagination, delusion, self-deception, wishful-thinking, emotionalism, sheer nonsense. And who shall gainsay them? 'The love of Jesus, what it is/None but his loved ones know.' I have seen no ghostly visions, and I have heard no mysterious voices; yet all that I have learned about Jesus has captivated my imagination with a dancing magic, utterly different in essence from the fascination which many other great historical figures hold for me.

His life and teaching speak immediately to the idealism that haunts man in every age. The blessedness of the meek (who possess immense strength kept humbly under perfect control) . . . the importance of forgiveness and reconciliation . . . the implications of 'Our Father' . . . that precious insight about serving (washing one another's feet) being the criterion of true greatness . . . the necessity of esteeming others more highly than oneself.

The story of his passion and death has a peculiar power which the centuries have heightened rather than diminished; and the drama of the resurrection (whatever you make of it) retains its ability to hit home with a strong, if tantalizing, impact. Here we approach the heart of the mystery, for it is this immediacy, this timelessness about Jesus, which is the secret of the mystical relationship. Again, I do not understand the psychological processes involved, neither do they interest me very much: but I believe that it is possible to be in love with Jesus today – not in love with a shadow or a memory, but with a contemporary power able to work in us something of the beauty we saw in him.

Jesus is never in the past. There is a dimension of eternity in everything we know of him. He is always being born, always healing, always saying 'Son, thy sins be forgiven thee', always turning water into wine, always walking on the waves, always speaking tenderly to Mary Magdalen, always washing the feet of his followers, always lying on the breast of the beloved disciple, always suffering, always dying, always rising again.

To glimpse his beauty, to taste his love, to acknowledge his attraction, and truly to desire him is to enter that mystical relation-

ship which is so hard to describe without sliding into sentimentality. 
Yet even that danger should not unduly alarm us. We do not weigh our words carefully when we speak with our beloved: nor should we worry when we express our love for our Lord. What if he is the Rose of Sharon, the Lily of the Valleys? Such is the language of poetry and of love. 'My beloved spake, and said unto me, Rise up, my love, my fair one, and come away . . .' Irrespective of differences which may on other issues divide them, this true love of Jesus draws into close intimacy all who have experienced the attraction and share the secret.

Over the altar in the chapel of the Little Portion Mission House (near my home) are painted the words: JESUS, JESUS ONLY, JESUS ALWAYS, JESUS IN ALL THINGS. How's that for a New Year resolution?

I enjoyed a spectacular new television production of *The Yeomen of the Guard*.

*Thursday 2 January*

We went on our longest route this morning – a circuitous, fifty-five miles to King's Lynn. I saw several patches of gorse in full flower, and imagined the scent (which epitomizes, for me, the flavour of heathland on warm, sunny days).

I saw a Celtic drunk at lunchtime, continuing his New Year celebrations. He was staggering along the road alone, swilling and spilling beer from a large Party-Four can – which struck me as particularly poignant.

Today I was gently accused of occasionally giving people the impression that I had no time for them. Apologies followed, but they were too late. The judgment was a harsh one, but I was horrified chiefly by the fact that I knew it was partly true. In a way, it dramatized the irony of my present mode of life. As a 'full-time' minister I had time I would have given gladly to people like those who often seek me now, but I was too far from them and they didn't come. I am near them now, and there is scarcely time to fit everyone in; the longer I continue the more difficult it becomes. My two-year juggling act as chairman of the branch was the most impossible period of all, and I hurt several people by my unavailability. Only Molly, my wife, really knows how much has to be fitted into each day. Sometimes it is literally true that I have no time for people. The bilocation of the saints is a secret I have yet to learn. But I try

GOD WAS IN CHRI

desperately hard to appear unhurried. Sometimes, evidently, I fail. 

Christian marriage is a permanent and life-long union – the formation of a family unit which only the trust and mutual respect of an irrevocable commitment can produce. The disadvantages – chiefly the loss of 'freedom' – are self-evident, but many (myself decidedly among them) would suggest that these are dwarfed by the benefits of belonging to the mini-community which is the family.

The exclusive nature of the marriage covenant, however, can introduce a tightness into the institution, and paradoxically threaten the unique relationship of love between husband and wife. Over the years, close relationships of affection and mutual understanding are liable to be forged with other men and women, by both husband and wife: one should expect and hope for this to happen. It does not imply 'running away' and deserting home, partner and children. It means that the world is full of fascinating people, with some of whom we fall in love. And in knowing, and loving, and trusting, and revealing, we ourselves are enriched: yes, and our homes and families are enriched in turn. The unique marriage bond does not consist solely in the sexual relationship, vital and central as that relationship most certainly is. Marriage is sexual union plus all the other unions and acts of sharing which go with it: economic union, domestic union, parenthood, commitment for life.

Our sexuality is the spring from which all our deepest friendships and true love-affairs flow (and how poor and mean our lives would be without them, even given marriage). The difficult question is this: how can these vital and proper extra-marital relationships find legitimate expression? A look . . . a smile . . . a casual touch . . . an arm round the waist or shoulder . . . eyes that sparkle knowingly . . . a dig in the ribs . . . a silence, tangible and pregnant with possibility . . . the ruffle of hair . . . a kiss . . . holding hands . . . words that can never be unsaid . . . more intimate touches . . . more abandoned kisses . . . sexual activity in all its varied, pleasurable forms . . .

At each extreme of this range of possibilities exist traditional viewpoints and ground upon which we feel reasonably secure: a look is usually all right – coition is all wrong! Between these extremes is a large area of uncharted territory in which (to put it mildly) we are not at ease. Is it, for example, wrong for persons of the same sex to embrace and kiss? If so, why? (Please don't suggest it is permissible for one sex, but not the other – unless you have very convincing reasons.) *Must* adultery be wrong in every possible circumstance?

All thoughtful persons realize there are few clear lines to be drawn through these matters. While nobody is demanding *An Ecclesiastical Handbook to the Human Anatomy*, it would be comforting to feel that theologians are giving these (and kindred) subjects realistic and urgent thought, because there is much confusion, and much ignorance, and much double-think. We seem to make very heavy weather of life, and through fear we cloud its gaiety, its joyfulness, and its spontaneity. We take ourselves much too seriously, and often overlook the element of the game, or the farce, which is never far away from the situations which together comprise our total human experience.

*Friday 3 January*

I typed an article and some letters this morning (my rest day), and played John Taverner's four-part Mass, 'The Western Wind', over and over again.

I must be hard to live with, sometimes; perhaps most of the time – especially during these bouts of self-analysis and introspection.

The small boy who spent New Year's Eve with us was on the bus this afternoon. He was accompanied by his granny, and his piping voice could be heard everywhere:

Jason: 'When the light is red, you can go.'

Granny: 'No, when it's red you've got to stop.'

Jason (with great emphasis): 'My – daddy – say, "When that's red, you go!".'

Me: 'And that's certainly how he drives his bus!'

I baptized Jason.

In the pub tonight I was accused of being schizophrenic. I'm not sure what compliment was intended, but I thought about the charge. I try, consciously and deliberately, to hold together and embody certain concepts and attitudes which I believe to have been rudely and unnaturally put asunder:

1. As a 'worker-priest' I am committed equally to the church and to the world – now in a black cassock, now in blue uniform.

2. This way of life is my personal response to the ecclesiastical realities of the twentieth century; yet I am a lover of history and tradition.

3. I serve in an ecumenical situation, and appear at one time in an Anglican setting, and next in one staunchly Nonconformist – wearing either hat with equal facility.

4. If I may say so without inviting the gross misrepresentation of my friends (who else?), I attempt to combine in my attitudes the tenderness and passivity of human femininity with all the assertiveness of human masculinity, rejoicing in the fact that male and female 'ingredients' are combined in us all.

5. I try to be a faithful minister of the gospel; I am also a man. So although to some people I may appear to be one thing one moment and something different the next, and to want one thing now and something else tomorrow, I am not whirling completely out of control. It is simply that I refuse to believe our varied human experiences belong to different worlds. There is ridiculously little either/or in this life: that is the joy and the wonder and the generosity of it. It is usually a question of both/and. I think I am not schizophrenic (in the popular understanding of that term). I am struggling to apprehend and live knowingly within that ultimate truth which holds all experience and all existence in a glorious unity.

In any case, he was drunk.

*Saturday 4 January*

Female intuition is feline, and frightens me; men are like innocent little boys by comparison.

I saw a dead hedgehog and a dead blackbird lying close together in the road. The mild weather had undoubtedly awakened the hedgehog; the blackbirds are usually killed at sunrise when they swoop low and slowly across the road, as though still half asleep.

In a New Year sale I bought two very cheap records of late mediaeval patriotic songs and early carols. A marvellous bargain!

*Sunday 5 January*

As my New Year resolution was to slow down, do less, and try to listen more, I thought a good way to begin would be to take a few less services! Tony plays football in a Sunday league, so I went to watch a game this morning. (I attended eight o'clock communion first.) Tony is the centre-forward; his team won 2–1 and he scored both goals. He was robbed of his best goal (and hat-trick) by the referee. Tony went for a beautiful through ball, and was clearly fouled by a defender. With skill he regained his balance, kept control of the ball, and lobbed it over the head of the advancing 'keeper – and as he kicked it, the referee blew for the foul! The ball dropped neatly under the bar for a perfect goal. It was a very late whistle,

and a bad decision. The referee actually apologized to Tony, but I was livid! 

*Monday 6 January*
I was disappointed that my shift prevented me attending both Epiphany services at the cathedral – festal evensong and sung eucharist. I fit a fair amount round my driving, but you can't win them all. But I love the festivals of our Lord, particularly those which the free churches never taught me to celebrate: Epiphany, Ascension, Transfiguration. This year I had to offer my 'costly devotion' as I sat at the wheel of my bus.

*Tuesday 7 January*
Once or twice during my life I have reflected on how pleasant it might have been to have had a slightly more illustrious Christian name – something unusual or distinguished! Even 'John' would have been more dignified. But 'Jack'!

Now, however, I've come to terms with it; indeed, I would almost go so far as to say that I like the ring of it. I bracket it mentally with 'Adam', the first man and representative of our race. 'Jack' is the working-class, poor-man's version, and occurs in a string of popular names and phrases:
Jack and Jill; Jack Sprat, Jack and the Beanstalk; Jack-a-dandy; Jack-by-the-Hedge; Jumping Jack; jack-tar; jack o'lantern; jack-of-all-trades; jack-in-the-box; Jack Frost; jack-in-office; Jack Ketch; jack-knife; jack-plane; jack-pike; jack-snipe; jack-pot; cheap jack; cracker-jack; apple-jack; yellow-jack; black-jack; lumberjack; steeplejack; Union Jack; every man Jack; Jack be nimble, Jack be quick, Jack jump over the candlestick.

*Wednesday 8 January*
The second of my patron saints is D. H. Lawrence (1885–1930) – who shares the same obituary date (2 March) as John Wesley! Lawrence wrote four major novels which I place second only to holy writ; yet at twenty I had never heard of him! After the unsuccessful prosecution for obscenity of *Lady Chatterley's Lover*, I bought a copy of the book whose title was on everybody's lips – and was overwhelmed by the power, the beauty, the sensitivity, and the insight it revealed. I was filled with anger at the gamekeeper jokes which proliferated month after month (they seemed profane),

and I was astonished that nobody had thought to tell me of this man, or urged me to read his books.

The key to Lawrence is contained in a passage in one of his finest essays, A *Propos of Lady Chatterley's Lover*, written shortly before his death:

'There are many ways of knowing, there are many sorts of knowledge. But the two ways of knowing, for man, are knowing in terms of apartness, which is mental, rational, scientific, and knowing in terms of togetherness, which is religious and poetic. The Christian religion lost, in Protestantism finally, the togetherness with the universe, the togetherness of the body, the sex, the emotions, the passions, with the earth and sun and stars.

*'But relationship is threefold. First, there is the relation to the living universe. Then comes the relation of man to woman. Then comes the relation of man to man. And each is a blood-relationship, not mere spirit or mind.'*

The first relationship finds expression throughout Lawrence's writings. These vibrate with an awareness and 'togetherness' which is far more than a mixture of keen observation and accurate description. It is felt when Mrs Morel sees the lilies and phlox in her garden at night, in *Sons and Lovers*. It is seen in the essay mentioned above in the passage beginning: 'The rhythm of the cosmos is something we cannot get away from, without bitterly impoverishing our lives.' It is illustrated best in *The Rainbow*, a chronicle of a farming family in the Midlands – a story of the soil told in almost biblical rhythms, and acclaimed by the critics as Lawrence's best novel.

The second relationship is described by Rupert Birkin in *Women in Love* when he tells Ursula: 'What I want is a strange conjunction with you . . . an equilibrium, a pure balance of two single beings: – as the stars balance each other.' Later, she asserts that he has said he wanted submission, to which he replies: 'I did not say, nor imply, a satellite. I meant two single equal stars balanced in conjunction.' Lawrence's deepest conviction was that men and women had broken 'the true pact between the body and soul', and in a serious attempt to bring them back into a balanced relationship he wrote *Lady Chatterley's Lover*:

'In the short summer night she learnt so much. She would have thought a woman would have died of shame. Instead of which, the shame died. Shame, which is fear . . .'

Lawrence's attitude is clear: 'The essential blood-contact is between man and woman, always has been so, always will be. The contact of positive sex.' 

But Lawrence had a word to add concerning the third relationship. He claimed that all three great relationships had become bodiless and dead. 'None, however, is quite so dead as the man-to-man relationship' – and this deadness is demonstrated by Gerald Crich and Rupert Birkin in *Women in Love*:

' "You've got to take down the love-and-marriage ideal from its pedestal. We want something broader. I believe in the additional perfect relationship between man and man – additional to marriage".

"I can never see how they can be the same," said Gerald.

"Not the same – but equally important, equally creative, equally sacred, if you like." '

Birkin – married to Ursula – wanted a real, ultimate relationship with Gerald; he wanted two kinds of love. Ursula rejected this longing as an obstinacy, a theory, a perversity, false, impossible.

For his handling of these immense and vital themes I regard David Herbert Lawrence with an admiration akin to awe. Like the gamekeeper, Mellors, he possessed the courage of his own tenderness: and fear has almost eliminated that quality from our enigmatic society which imagines itself liberated.

' "Ay! it's tenderness really . . . Sex is really only touch, the closest of all touch. And it's touch we're afraid of. We're only half-conscious, and half alive. We've got to come alive and aware. Especially the English have got to get into touch with one another, a bit delicate and a bit tender. It's our crying need." '

*Thursday 9 January*

When I walked into the canteen this morning before starting my shift, no less than four people approached me – one after the other – to discuss what might be termed 'pastoral matters'. I wanted to speak to my conductor, but couldn't reach him! Such excessive 'demand' is unusual, but few days pass without a number of these conversations.

The daylight seemed to linger a moment longer this afternoon, and for the first time this winter I felt that the days were lengthening.

*Friday 10 January*

Monica Furlong:

'As we grow older love becomes more diffuse . . . I find myself longing to tell all sorts of people that I love them. And people say it much more to me than in the days when I longed to hear it. When you can say it, and hear it without assuming that love is about possession, it is wonderful how rich all relationships become.'[1]

*Saturday 11 January*

I live in the most interesting street in the city; so, at least, I maintain. Barely five hundred yards in length, it boasts three mediaeval churches and two of the historic meeting houses of Europe – plus a dozen other buildings of outstanding historical and architectural interest. The derivation of the street-name – Colegate – is obscure, and although the termination 'gate' is Danish, the thoroughfare probably originated as a Saxon track beside the river. Today it displays the architectural styles of five hundred years: fifteenth-century flint churches; a sixteenth-century merchant's house; seventeenth-century dog-toothed gables; eighteenth-century classical elegance; a Victorian shoe-factory; and twentieth-century award-winning town houses. At the east end of the street is St Clement's, which guards the tomb of the parents of Elizabeth I's Archbishop of Canterbury, Matthew Parker, who preached here. Halfway along the street stands St George's, a noble building full of interesting features and the resting-place of one of the greatest English landscape painters, John Crome. At the west end of Colegate is St Michael's, which has two chantry chapels and some of the best flint flushwork in the country. Between St Clement's and St George's – and almost within touching distance – stand The Octagon Chapel and The Old Meeting House. The Octagon was visited and described by John Wesley in 1757 – the year after it was opened: 'I was shewn Dr Taylor's new Meeting House, perhaps the most elegant one in Europe. It is eight square, built of the finest brick, with sixteen sash windows below, as many above, and eight sky lights in the dome which are indeed purely ornamental. The inside is furnished in the highest taste, and is as clean as any nobleman's saloon. The Communion table is fine mahogany; the very latches of the pew-doors are polished brass. How can it be thought that the old coarse Gospel should find admission here?' The Octagon Chapel was described by Southey as 'The Vatican of the Unitarian hierarchy'; between 1775 and 1805 it was unquestionably one of

[1] Monica Furlong, *Travelling In,* paperback ed., p. 37.

OCTAGON
CHAPEL

the chief intellectual centres in England, renowned for its scholarship, brilliance and wit. By comparison, The Old Meeting House is austere and dignified; built in 1693, it is the home of a congregation whose history is a stirring romance of excommunication, exile, and covenant. Its Dutch appearance and the Dutch clinker paving are a reminder of those early days, while another writer has commented: 'The atmosphere seems so redolent of New England that even in Norwich one instinctively looks round for the pine trees of the forest.' All this, and much more, is to be enjoyed in Colegate; not bad for five hundred yards!

*Sunday 12 January*

Two 'bus' baptisms.

I saw a very bright shooting star which seemed to hang in the sky for an instant before vanishing.

Some people are fun simply to be with.

*Monday 13 January*

At evensong I was moved by the singing of psalm 69 (which, at Norwich, is sung to settings by Teesdale and Hawes):

*Save me, O God: for the waters are come in, even unto my soul.*

*I stick fast in the deep mire, where no ground is: I am come into deep waters, so that the floods run over me.*

*Tuesday 14 January*

As I tidied the garden a thrush sang loudly in the ash tree, and a robin hopped near. I threw some soaked bread for him, but he was more appreciative of a grub I uncovered and tossed in his direction.

A pastoral visit I made this afternoon to a woman in her mid-sixties did more good to me than it did to her. She cheered me, and helped to correct my perspective. I was warmed by her compassion, her down-to-earth common sense, and her easy ability to separate important issues from the trivial, paltry matters which ultimately don't matter at all! Warmth and compassion and love and forgiveness and reconciliation and tenderness – these are what Christianity is about. It is all so much greater than ethical codes or disputes about the validity of non-episcopal orders. Christianity is about a freedom so immense it is frightening.

*My flesh and my heart faileth: but God is the strength of my heart, and my portion for ever.*

*Wednesday 15 January*
I saw a tortoiseshell butterfly fluttering round some roses this morning – how's that for mid-January!?

Conducted a funeral.

Two incidents occurred today which I felt I did not handle very well. I just do not pray enough; I am not receptive enough; and then I get caught slightly off balance.

*They spake against God also, saying: Shall God prepare a table in the wilderness?*

*Thursday 16 January*
The blackthorn is in blossom, looking like snow on the branches.

*Friday 17 January*
I was consulted at work today about a poltergeist, and a possible exorcism.

I enjoyed a driver's account of a recent conversation between his wife and small son:

'Mum, when I die, will I go to Jesus?'

'Yes, I expect so.'

'That's what I thought; after all, that's what he's there for.'

Evensong;
*My song shall be alway of the loving-kindness of the Lord: with my mouth will I ever be shewing thy truth from one generation to another.*

Frank, who was my conductor four years ago, called with his wife to see me tonight. The brother of another former conductor had called earlier, and later in the evening Roy – who hasn't yet left, after all – came to the pub (and tried loudly to expound his personal, complicated scheme to conquer inflation).

*Saturday 18 January*
Tony and I ran all the way from the garage to the football ground to see the match: ('You don't do too bad for your age' – cheeky young demon). York City scored after thirty-eight seconds. We were aghast! They scored again after ninety-five seconds. We were numbed and unbelieving! 'Good job we didn't miss the start,' muttered Tony. York all but made it three in three minutes – but we couldn't have been hurt any more. In the second half we pulled one back, but they scored a third goal. With only minutes remaining we made it 3–2, and that was the result – but how York City sur-

 vived the final onslaught I shall never know. I think this game had to be won; I fear it will cost us promotion.

*Sunday 19 January*
God has made us wonderfully different. With our varied equipment we perceive him differently, interpret his word differently, and respond to him in worship in a variety of ways. Our ritual – whatever form it takes – should be devised and intended to make God real, not remote; to reveal him, not to conceal him. For some of us this takes place most effectively in colourful ceremonies performed with scrupulous attention to the smallest detail (because only the best is good enough for God). For others, God is encountered most vividly and adored most lovingly in the simplest of forms. And most of us are somewhere in between.

Leaving aside theological considerations, the differences in human temperament will ensure that a variety of religious practices – with differences in doctrine, worship, ethos, and emphasis – will survive. And this is important not only because the church must cater for all types of people. It is important because we ourselves need variety in our religious diet (just as we need it in other areas of our experience). We are almost different people at different times. Our desires and emotions vary according to the time of day, the season of the year, the period of life, or the circumstances of the moment, and require new expressions and outlets.

Usually, we will find our spiritual home in one tradition which, by and large, ministers to our spiritual and emotional condition most completely: but there will be times (unless my experience is markedly different from yours) when a different church and another viewpoint and an unusual pattern of worship (even if unfamiliar almost to the point of being unintelligible!) will suddenly make God real, and near, and precious. That, at any rate, has been my experience. Not only are we different from one another; we ourselves are different, at different times.

When I was feeling depressed the other evening and went into St Clement's – lighting a couple of candles, filling the place full of incense, and waiting in silence for the gift of peace – my behaviour may not have seemed like that of a Methodist. It may have seemed more like a cross between Roman Catholicism and Quakerism! But I don't care *what* it seemed like. (To confuse you even more, I might add that I know as many old Sankey hymns as anyone who hast sayed the course and is still reading this book.) 

Those old labels have ceased to have the meaning that once they possessed, and younger Christians in particular are finding them irksome and unreal. I claim everything good in the history of the Christian church, from whatever branch or tradition, as part of my inheritance. Today, it is sometimes so hard to believe that I cannot afford to throw away anything carelessly out of the window which could help to quicken my devotion and bring me closer to God.

*Monday 20 January*
It rained steadily all day. I can still visualize my windscreen-wiper.

*Tuesday 21 January*
David is a conductor seldom seen in the canteen without a library book. Today, he showed me a delightful story in Pete Seeger's *The Incompleat Folksinger* concerning the wife of the Dutch governor of Bali who, late last century, compelled her husband to decree that women must wear clothing on the upper half of the body. The following Sunday, as the governor and his wife rode in their carriage to church, the populace lined up alongside the road. When the carriage approached, all the women raised their skirts and covered the upper half of their bodies.

*Wednesday 22 January*
Sorry to return to football so soon, but tonight's event must not pass unrecorded! We watched an exciting second-leg of a semi-final cup-tie. In the first-leg, Norwich City had drawn 2–2 with Manchester United at Old Trafford. Tonight's floodlit match – with a place at Wembley at stake – produced a tense struggle with plenty of cup-tie atmosphere, and Colin Suggett's goal in the fifty-fourth minute was enough to settle the match. The ball came over from a corner on the right; Suggett's header was pushed out, somebody else headed it back, it came out yet again, and Suggett threw himself forward to head the ball past the goalkeeper and into the net. Result: Norwich City 1, Manchester United 0.

*Thursday 23 January*
This month's book is *Free Fall* by William Golding. I agree with the critics that its moral honesty and cosmic splendour of vision prove it to be the work of an indisputable genius. The world of

Sammy Mountjoy was transmuted into a place of wonder, beauty, music, and love:

'I returned to my fourth dimension and found that love flows along it until the heart, the physical heart, this pump or alleged pump makes love as easy as a bee makes honey. This seemed to me at that time the only worth-while occupation; and while I was so engaged the pace became so hot that a flake of fire, a brightness, flicked out of the hidden invisible and settled on the physical heart for all the world as though the heart is what poetry thinks it to be and not just a bit of clever machinery . . . All these things, of course, were explicable in two ways; the one explained them away, the other accepted them as data relevant to the nature of the cosmos. There was no argument possible between people holding either view.'[1]

*Friday 24 January*

As it was my rest day I was able to watch the enthronement of the Archbishop of Canterbury on television. The sheer splendour of the occasion enthralled me, and a personal touch of poignancy was provided by memories of the last occasion on which such a service was held, when I was present in the cathedral at Canterbury. I even remember Archbishop Ramsey's text: 'And there went with him a band of men, whose hearts God had touched' (I Sam. 10.26). There can't be many people who have attended the enthronement service of the Primate of All England – while on honeymoon!

*I will keep thy ceremonies: O forsake me not utterly.*

*Saturday 25 January*

Christians have a right – frequently, a duty – to accept promotion and the greater responsibilities which attend it. Staff-jobs are advertised occasionally at work which would tempt me – were I free to be tempted. But there will be no promotion for me. I am providing a Christian presence at shop-floor level; for that reason, questions of increased income, security, and responsibility simply do not arise. I am there for other reasons.

*Sunday 26 January*

Today's tiny congregations impressed upon me yet again the immensity of the rejection of formal church attendance by the people.

[1] William Golding, *Free Fall*, Faber & Faber 1959, pp. 187f. Reprinted by permission.

The reasons have been analysed many times, but wherever will it end? A people without religion – and with precious little to take its place.

For all that, I sense a strange exhilaration in the air, particularly away from 'religious' people. I disapprove strongly of much I see in modern society – the erosion of respect for any form of authority, the disturbing spread of violence – but there is much that is good and hopeful. Even the dabbling in drugs and the occult is evidence of a hunger and longing. The young – with an economic independence undreamt of a few years ago – are especially stimulating, while the new interest in meditation and prayer has, if anything, exposed still more of our hollowness and superficiality. A wistful affection for the church (or for the dimension of 'otherness') is seen in the crowds which flock to the Christmas midnight mass in increasing numbers. The new sexual openness; the idealism which finds expression in action for the aged, homeless, and refugees; the sense of freedom which has well-nigh destroyed all the traditional taboos and restraints these contribute to the invigorating flavour of modern society. It is no mean privilege to bear the name of Christ at such a time. In so many places the church is literally dying out. I wonder what God will do? I wonder what he is doing already? Of one thing we may be confident. The widespread collapse of 11 a.m. and 6.30 p.m. does not signify the collapse of God.

*Monday 27 January*

As I walked home from work at six this evening through dark, wet back-streets, I became conscious that a bird was singing nearby, loudly, in the heart of the city, an hour after darkness had fallen. I was glad.

*Tuesday 28 January*

At evensong I was moved by one of my favourite psalms: psalm 137, sung to the setting by Lloyd in G:

*By the waters of Babylon we sat down and wept: when we remembered thee, O Sion.*
*As for our harps, we hanged them up: upon the trees that are therein.*
*For they that led us away captive required of us then a song, and melody, in our heaviness: Sing us one of the songs of Sion.*
*How shall we sing the Lord's song: in a strange land?*
*If I forget thee, O Jerusalem: let my right hand forget her cunning.*

 *If I do not remember thee, let my tongue cleave to the roof of my mouth: yea, if I prefer not Jerusalem in my mirth.*

*Wednesday 29 January*

The gardens really belong at the moment not to the unseasonable marigolds and red-hot-pokers, but to the snowdrops and elephant's ears, which are at their best.

I saw a school playing-field which contained a large number of fieldfares and redwings. In a nearby beech wood, flocks of bramblings mingled with chaffinches and sparrows.

*Thursday 30 January*

I have two pet dislikes: back-slappers and plastic flowers.

Sometimes, I think I am the kind of person to whom no bread is better than half a loaf.

*Friday 31 January*

*Let every thing that hath breath: praise the Lord.*

Throughout evensong I gazed at the great Norman arches; their simple beauty and immense strength were profoundly reassuring. They emphasized my smallness and transience, yet raised my thinking into adoration.

*Saturday 1 February*

This was an ordinary kind of day from which those two imposters, triumph and disaster, remained aloof. Yet why should a day be called ordinary when it contained good companionship, satisfying work, laughter, wholesome food, and much more beside? The day was shot through with the goodness of God, and I called it ordinary! Then thank God for the 'ordinary-ness' of life: that each day is so laden with riches that we forget how wealthy we are. It is in a day like today that God is most likely to be perceived and enjoyed. What we dismiss as ordinary proves often, upon more thoughtful examination, to be not so ordinary after all.

*Sunday 2 February*

A superb Candlemas Day. The bright sunlight, the crisp air, the spectacular sunset and the evening mist awakened the body from the inertia of winter (like a creature stirring from hibernation); the senses were alerted, and strained to capture and experience all that the day had to offer. Today I was conscious of being alive!

I conducted morning worship, and worked a late shift. Fog came down tonight. I happen to believe that bus-drivers earn every penny they receive in modern traffic conditions – but they earn it twice over in fog. Two quotations to show how circumstances alter cases:

'Sorry we're late, but we got stuck behind a bus . . .'

'Sorry we're late, but the fog was bad – we could hardly see a thing, so we stuck behind a bus . . .'

*Monday 3 February*

Although it seems that many of our traditional freedoms are being taken gradually from us, we can – for the time being, at least! – still think our thoughts and dream our dreams and let our imaginations run riot. A lively imagination is a wonderful gift. It sets us free from physical restrictions, and enables us to travel through time and space, meeting people we never knew, reviving memories stored deeply away, and leaving us richer and more experienced.

I like to change the season sometimes (always we pine for whatever it is we don't happen to possess at the moment!). I came along Magdalen Street on a chilly afternoon recently, about five o'clock, and decided I would change the month. I thought for a moment, and selected the end of June. And there it was! No overcoats buttoned at the top, no scarves, no cold puddles. It wasn't dark, and the traffic had no glaring headlights. My imagination had taken care of all those things! It was nearly tea-time on a summer afternoon; the early-evening sun was shining brightly, and women wore summer dresses. It was warm, and there were several holiday-makers about. A bus was taking children home from school, their satchels full of books for exam revision, and cricket and tennis gear; a long, bright evening stretched before them. Then my imagination collapsed – and suddenly, it was winter again!

*Tuesday 4 February*

The providing of hospitality and the serving of meals is a sacred activity. As my dinner appeared on the table today, the simplicity of the familiar ritual seemed transfigured, and I understood that what I was being offered truly was not simply food; I was being given a few hours more of life.

'I like coming to your house. It is one place that never seems to change. Everything is always the same – and, somehow, that's rather comforting.' Those words gave us pleasure.

Having learnt by heart the name of every football ground in the English and Scottish Leagues, we have turned temporarily to rhymes and couplets. Tony's best offering tonight was:

She was only the barmaid's daughter –
But she knew how to pull a fast one.

The Union chairman of another branch sought me out to ask my opinion on a certain matter.

*Wednesday 5 February*

The yellow crocuses are the first to flower and can be seen now in many gardens. It is light in the afternoons until well after five o' clock. Our thrush continues to sing at full volume morning and evening – and most of the day, as well. He perches on the same twig at the very top of the ash tree.

*Thursday 6 February*

Life is very beautiful and infinitely mysterious. Meditation and sex and religion and love are closely interwoven. Music and painting and literature beckon towards new dimensions of experience. Each day is a gift.

*Friday 7 February*

Occasionally, I feel I am in spiritual peril, and hope desperately that I am being prayed for. I am not protected by the padding of an ecclesiastical routine; I am pitifully exposed to the world – much more than a layman, for I am acknowledged as an accredited representative. I am fearful lest my witness should flag, and my charity fail. The longer I remain in the world, the greater the danger grows. I must cling to piety and integrity without becoming aloof; I must be sympathetic and human without conforming utterly to 'worldly' attitudes. I walk a tight-rope, and my unaided temperament would have betrayed me long ago – my weaknesses are legion. I do not suffer fools gladly, yet must never be wanting in patience or compassion. I must guard constantly against meeting pettiness with pettiness. How easily I could be thrown, and destroyed.

*Saturday 8 February*

An exciting and full-blooded football match against West Bromwich Albion. The score went 0–1, 1–1, 1–2, 2–2, 3–2! This was the game at its best – and winning made it even sweeter!

*Sunday 9 February*

Bear with me then, if lawful what I ask:
Love not the heav'nly spirits, and how their love
Express they? by looks only? or do they mix
Irradiance, virtual or immediate touch?
   To whom the angel, with a smile that glow'd
Celestial rosy red, love's proper hue,
Answer'd: Let it suffice thee that thou know'st
Us happy, and without love no happiness.
Whatever pure thou in the body enjoy'st
(And pure thou wert created,) we enjoy
In eminence, and obstacle find none
Of membrane, joint, or limb, exclusive bars;
Easier than air with air, if spirits embrace,
Total they mix, union of pure with pure
Desiring; nor restrain'd conveyance need,
As flesh to mix with flesh, or soul with soul.

John Milton, *Paradise Lost, Book VIII*
(Spoken by Adam and Raphael)

*Monday 10 February*

A tantalizing day. I went to Breydon, but a thick fog refused to lift. I could hear plenty of wild-fowl, and glimpsed some wild swans, but saw little else. Later, I passed a garden where a hollyhock was in flower.

*Tuesday 11 February*

Shrove Tuesday; I was feasted with pancakes.

*He shall dwell before God for ever: O prepare thy loving mercy and faithfulness, that they may preserve him.*

*So will I alway sing praise unto thy Name: that I may daily perform my vows.*

*Wednesday 12 February*

Ash Wednesday.

Work – funeral – evensong. Penitential psalms 102, 130, 142: *For I have eaten ashes as it were bread: and mingled my drink with weeping.*

As a Lenten discipline I intend to read aloud one chapter of Isaiah in church each day. I intend also to read *Agape and Eros* by Anders Nygren.

*Thursday 13 February*

An old man I visited declared that the human body was a marvellous thing, and added: 'God must have been a wonderful man.'

*I will praise the Name of God with a song: and magnify it with thanksgiving.*

*Friday 14 February*

St Valentine – an important festival! (Tony received an anonymous and slightly rude Valentine, about which he kept very quiet. I can't imagine who sent it.)

*Saturday 15 February*

This afternoon I was overtaken by a large, dirty tanker. In the dry mud on the rear panel somebody had written with their finger: 'What kind of fuel am I?'

The sunshine of late afternoon and early evening, with its distinctive mellowness and long shadows, has the ability to transfigure the most unsightly surroundings. In the full glare of mid-day there are many streets and districts which I find unappealing – sometimes stark, sometimes ugly. On a sunny evening, however, everything is changed. The spirit of the area – what it means to live there – becomes tangible, and the unlikeliest places are found to possess a charm of their own.

*Sunday 16 February*

This month's book is *Claudine at School* by Colette.

*Monday 17 February*

Pierre Hamp, a French socialist writer:

'The tradition of Jesus the Carpenter, of Paul the Carpetmaker has no continuity . . . The priest limits himself to his parliamentary role; he discourses. He doesn't do his day's work at the machines. With him, as with all those that insist on keeping their hands clean, the contempt for work shows not so much by words but by lack of contact. They praise work and keep away from it. The separation between the church and working life has been achieved by priests with clean hands, renegades from the religion in which the first disciples and Saint Paul were in communion.'[1]

*Tuesday 18 February*

I made three short contributions to the discussions at my branch meeting. I was accused afterwards of swaying the vote, but my former colleagues on the platform seemed grateful.

*Wednesday 19 February*

February can produce some of the most invigorating days of the whole year, when the sun combines the warmth of early summer with the freshness and promise of spring. This was such a day; the sunshine flowed through my veins (what matter if I was in my cab most of the time?) and made it good to be alive.

*Thursday 20 February*

Monica Furlong makes a pertinent and courageous admission: 'I like the thread of thought that runs through Christian thinking about sanctity, that holiness includes a liberation of the body as well as of the spirit.'

Antinomianism is the heretical view that Christians are by grace set free from the need of observing any moral law. That is the pitfall, and that would be the charge levelled at anyone imprudent enough to suggest too strongly that 'the glorious liberty of the sons of God' includes a physical emancipation. But it is true.

Few thanks, however, in church or world, await the person who says so. For a man or woman to approach within a foot of a person of the opposite sex is a clear indication to the Christian mind that a family is about to be betrayed and deserted, or a hideous sin committed. For people of the same sex to express affection is incontrovertible evidence of unspeakable perversion.

Christ Almighty! Bottle up your love! Kill it, hide it, do what you like with it, *so long as you don't show it*! Lawrence, we need you more than ever. Our love has become so small. It doesn't really matter that warmth is forbidden: there isn't much left to express. Where does liberty end and antinomianism begin?

*Friday 21 February*

Two strikingly similar quotations which seem to take the discussion

[1] Henri Perrin, *Priest and Worker: An Autobiography*, Macmillan 1965, p. 89.

a little further, illustrating fear of physical closeness – and the consequences:

'I went to see her in the nursing-home. They had pumped her out and she was feeling much better. She came down to meet me in the gothic hall and took me to her room. She was beautifully dressed, and her finger-nails were painted, and she made me feel rather a mess. Her room was full of flowers, my own among them, and the nurse brought in tea, and stayed to chat. We were sorry when she went, because the conversation dragged. I was embarrassed that she had attempted suicide, and did not know whether to refer to it or not. She talked about the viscount in the next room.

When I stood up to go she suddenly broke down and said that now her lover had left her she could not go on. She could not go home if his body was not beside her in the bed. She felt totally alone.

I knew what she was asking of me at that moment – to take her in my arms and be her mother. But I was afraid – of making a fool of myself (she had always had an acid tongue), and perhaps of the sexual implications of embracing a woman. And I was in a hurry – I wanted to get away before the rush-hour traffic got too bad – and there were old resentments between us which had never quite healed. So I said something non-committal and went away.

A few weeks later she killed herself. I had not stabbed or shot her, nor administered the tablets which poisoned her. But I had let her starve before my eyes.'[1]

'I never told this to anybody before, and I really don't know why I'm telling you. It's just that the last time I saw Rufus, before he disappeared . . . we had a fight, he said he was going to kill me. And, at the very end, when he was finally in bed, after he'd cried, and after he'd told me – so many terrible things – I looked at him, he was lying on his side, his eyes were half open, he was looking at me. I was taking off my pants . . . and I was going to stay there, I was afraid to leave him alone. Well, when he looked at me, just before he closed his eyes and turned on his side away from me, all curled up, I had the weirdest feeling that he wanted me to take him in my arms. And not for sex, though maybe sex would have happened. I had the feeling that he wanted someone to hold him, to hold him, and that, that night, it had to be a man. I got in the bed and I thought about it and I watched his back . . . and I lay

[1] Monica Furlong, *Travelling In*, paperback ed., pp. 31–2.

on my back and I didn't touch him and I didn't sleep. I remember that night as a kind of vigil. I don't know whether he slept or not, I kept trying to tell from his breathing – but I couldn't tell, it was too choppy, maybe he was having nightmares. I loved Rufus, I loved him. I didn't want him to die. But when he was dead, I thought about it, thought about it – isn't it funny? I didn't know I'd thought about it as much as I have – and I wondered, I guess I still wonder, what would have happened if I'd taken him in my arms, if I'd held him, if I hadn't been – afraid. I was afraid that he wouldn't understand that it was – only love. Only love. But, oh, Lord, when he died, I thought that maybe I could have saved him if I'd just reached out that quarter of an inch between us on that bed, and held him . . . Do you know what I mean? I haven't told Ida this, I haven't told anyone, I haven't thought about it, since he died. But I guess I've been living with it. And I'll never know. I'll never know.'[1]

What do we make of all that? Must the word be made flesh? The closer we grow to Christ, the less inhibited we should become. Our hearts should overflow with love – at least, our hymns say so. But surely that doesn't mean that affection and warmth should find so much as a hint of physical expression?! Prayer, O.K. Service to the community, yes. Sacrificial giving, sure – this is the meaning of Christian love; but actually to touch . . .!

*Saturday 22 February*

This morning I acted as subdeacon at a solemn requiem mass, and sang a lesson from the Revelation of St John the Divine. I am perfectly happy to genuflect, and to kiss the altar in a greeting to God; candles and incense are a delight after long draughts of Nonconformity at its most dreary; the entire service was a joy, and I shared in it without theological reservation. It soared beyond names and sects and parties. The mass was offered in thanksgiving for the life of John Godolphin Bennett (1897–1974), philosopher, writer, and exponent of the teachings of Georges Gurdjieff.

By an unexpected coincidence there was more incense this evening: I attended a memorable production of Peter Luke's *Hadrian VII*.

[1] James Baldwin, *Another Country*, Michael Joseph 1963, pp. 329f.

*Sunday 23 February*

Everything else being equal, I get on fairly well with children, teenagers, the mentally retarded, the sick, the elderly, and the bereaved. I am noticeably less at ease with people who are well-off, and people who are very clever. Perhaps I like to be in charge, and am happy with those over whom I can lord it and insecure with those who can lord it over me. Or, perhaps, wealth and academic ability create their own particular barriers. I have felt more at home in prison (and I hate prisons) than at certain social gatherings. It is a weakness, I know; but it is hard to shake off.

*Monday 24 February*

St Clement's is floodlit tonight, as usual. The bare, graceful ailanthus in the churchyard is silhouetted against the tower, and a fog has come down and surrounded the building. From my attic window the view is bewitching – like peering into a beautiful peep-show.

My younger daughter, Jeanette, aged six, brought me a poem she had written:

At night I see the moon
Peeping into the window
And I see the moon's face
In the silent night.

*Tuesday 25 February*

This has been a good winter for bramblings; never before have I noticed so many. The cock bird in winter plumage is strikingly handsome, with jet-black head and orange/gold breast and wings. The black-headed gulls are beginning to show their spring plumage. With dark, chocolate-brown heads they, too, look elegant.

*Wednesday 26 February*

Another quotation from *Another Country*:

'No, I don't think I'm in love with her. I love her very much, we get on beautifully together. But she's not all tangled up in my guts the way I guess Ida is all tangled up in yours.'

*Thursday 27 February*

There was a slight frost and some thick fog early this morning. When, eventually, the sun forced its way through, it lighted on the delicate tracery of hedges covered with hoar-frost. I was thrilled, and realized afresh that there is never a plus without a minus. We have been glad to escape with a winter of unprecedented mildness – yet there has been one great loss. No winter, no beauty. No treacherous driving conditions, but no snowscapes, no icicles, no frost-covered window-panes. 

*They that sow in tears: shall reap in joy.*

*He that now goeth on his way weeping, and beareth forth good seed: shall doubtless come again with joy, and bring his sheaves with him.*

*Friday 28 February*

We did the King's Lynn trip again, in fog.

London Underground railway disaster at Moorgate.

*For though the Lord be high, yet hath he respect unto the lowly: as for the proud, he beholdeth them afar off.*

*Saturday 1 March*

An illustration of Norfolk temperament:

At Wembley today the seat next but one to mine was occupied by a man I recognized the moment he arrived. I cannot recall having met him since we left school nineteen years ago. He greeted me warmly: 'Hello, Jack, you old devil; are you all right?' 'Not too bad,' I replied, 'how are you?' And that was that! I was with Trevor, he was with some companions; we grimaced once or twice during the game (in which Aston Villa humiliated Norwich), and said 'Mind how you go' at the end, but there was no long conversation. This did not, however, denote a basic lack of sympathy. It's just our way; our reunions in heaven will probably be equally taciturn (though one must trust that the form of brief greeting will be suitably amended).

Incidentally, it's a terrible thing to watch your favourite team lose at Wembley.

*Sunday 2 March*

Under the eaves of a tiny cottage next to The Bell at Salhouse is written, in Gothic letters, the words 'God's Providence is Mine Inheritance.' Local legend asserts that during an outbreak of plague, this was the only house in the village which escaped unvisited. I reflect on those words each time I go through Salhouse, and record them here as a text appropriate for the day on which this diary reaches its half-way mark! 'God's Providence is Mine Inheritance.'

*Monday 3 March*

To my great annoyance, Tony injured his leg playing football yesterday, and the doctor has put him on the club for a week! I shall have an assortment of conductors until he comes back.

*Tuesday 4 March*

Suddenly, it's spring – though, in truth, there has been no winter. Now the gardens are filled with daffodils and wallflowers. The strange mixture of the seasons was epitomized in the sunshine of this afternoon when I noticed a group of blue hyacinths, behind which was a climbing-rose with two perfectly-formed pink blooms. The pink and blue blended affectingly.

*The Lord is my shepherd: therefore can I lack nothing.*

*Wednesday 5 March*

A large flock of gulls in a field, all standing perfectly still and all facing the same direction . . .

*Thursday 6 March*

At the terminus two girls from Lancashire boarded the bus. The conductor soon chatted them up and said, pointing to me: 'I don't suppose you know he's a vicar?' To which one of the girls replied instantly: 'That's funny – we're both nuns. They've just let us out!' I thought that a very witty and worthy rejoinder.

How important it is that Christians should witness to their faith – but sometimes the witness is a mixed one. Today I was cut-up by a car which displayed a sticker in the rear window: YOU NEED CHRIST. Within the sanctuary of my cab I answered aloud, irritably: 'Not if he can't teach me to drive better than that.'

*Friday 7 March*

I noticed some crocuses which had pushed through a tarmac path.

I visited the overgrown ruins of an old hall. Royalty was entertained here on many occasions, and the hall and grounds retain a strong, melancholy influence as though their former glory belonged not to some distant age but to a different dimension. Time is a curious phenomenon: past, present and future swirl inseparably together.

*Keep innocency, and take heed unto the thing that is right: for that shall bring a man peace at the last.*

*Saturday 8 March*
Driving on a country route I saw coltsfoot and red dead nettle in flower.

*Sunday 9 March*
Mothering Sunday. Worked an early shift and conducted evening worship.

*Monday 10 March*
An old man, off for a day's fishing, boarded the bus with a long set of rods. Greatly to my amusement, the first thing he caught today was Tony's ear.

*O cast thy burden upon the Lord, and he shall nourish thee: and shall not suffer the righteous to fall for ever.*

*Tuesday 11 March*
A spoilt meal is a minor tragedy. (Perhaps the potatoes are burnt, or the phone rings, or someone is in a hurry, or a quarrel has left an atmosphere.) The Last Supper was a spoilt meal.

*Hear my crying, O God: give ear unto my prayer.*
*From the ends of the earth will I call upon thee: when my heart is in heaviness.*

*Wednesday 12 March*
Young people are good company and their influence, as I've remarked, can be powerful. For example, I have observed middle-aged bus-drivers, not noted for cheerfulness, displaying new brightness when they have been detailed to work with young conductors. The change has been swift and surprising. Most youngsters possess this contagious zest because the world lies at their feet. They are not old enough to have become disillusioned. They have plans and hopes. For them, it is always springtime. Life is an unfolding mystery – frightening, challenging, immensely exciting – and they have not yet lost the (very religious) ability to wonder. Knowledge and discovery, friendship and love, work and music, new sexual self-awareness: it is from these that the gladdening, irresistable, infectious vibrations flow, which we who are older find sweet after life's bitterness, and invigorating amid the responsibilities imposed by the years. How could anyone be unaffected in the presence of such hope, and unmoved by such unclouded promise?

I have hinted, too, at the other side of the story: in contrast, how dull and lifeless, uninteresting and restricted, many mature adults become. To work with them can be an ordeal. Life (which may, of course, have treated them badly) has lost its savour, and wonder has died. There is nothing to talk about, for something vital within them has burnt itself out. Worst of all is the speed with which the promise of youth slides into the stolidity of adulthood. The responsibilities of marriage and parenthood appear often to set the process in motion. Perhaps it is inevitable. Personally, I do not believe so. I believe it is unspeakably sad.

Certainly, we ought not to seek an escape, a perpetual immaturity, a Peter Pan existence; childishness in adults is embarrassing. But that sense of hope, promise, excitement, expectancy, wonder, awe, and reverence – with the sheer joy of being alive – this is something that need not be surrendered with the passing of the years.

*Thursday 13 March*

*But, Lord, I make my prayer unto thee: in an acceptable time.*

I saw a tawny owl in a quiet city street; it was perched on a television aerial, and hooting.

This month I have spent much time protesting! I have protested against the proposed redundancy of St Clement's (where I spend many hours of quietness in the course of a year), and I have protested against the construction of a miniature golf-course on land which is, to all intents and purposes, part of the heath. 'They' can't leave anything alone, these days. I am not a rich man (in the material sense of that word); the things I enjoy most belong to everyone: an old church . . . the heath . . . an over-grown cemetery . . . a group of ancient cottages. Then someone decides to change them needlessly, or tidy them, or pull them down. Not that my protests achieve anything! On the contrary – my espousal of a cause proves unfailingly to be the kiss of death.

*Friday 14 March*

*Nevertheless, I am alway by thee: for thou hast holden me by my right hand.*

*Thou shalt guide me with thy counsel: and after that receive me with glory.*

*Saturday 15 March*

I attended the spring concert presented by my old school. The highlight of the evening was the return of two old boys who played Vivaldi's Concerto in G Minor for Two Cellos and played also in the Requiem for Three Cellos and Piano by Popper. The programme concluded with Vivaldi's 'Gloria'. 

*Sunday 16 March*
'The virtues of Youth are much exaggerated. You are vain, ruthless, shallow, ignorant of the precipice upon which you stand, and unacquainted with grief' – Eric Ashley in *Lord Dismiss Us* by Michael Campbell (Corgi 1968).

*Monday 17 March*
The rooks are back at the rookery, inspecting and repairing. There were wintry showers this morning, and at lunchtime I brought Linda, my elder daughter, home from school in heavy snow. She was very excited, laughing and squealing all the way; and I must confess that I was excited, too. The showers exhausted themselves this afternoon.

British Summer Time commenced yesterday, and it was a pleasure to drive through the evening rush-hour tonight in sunshine. I like the tea-time peak-period on a bright afternoon. For most people the day's work is over, and they are looking forward to getting home and enjoying the evening. It is the antithesis of a wet morning!

*Tuesday 18 March*
The daffodils on the castle mound are a picture. Tony said the illuminated castle was one of the most impressive sights of which he knew. Certainly, the citizens of Norwich are fortunate to have such a noble back-cloth against which to live and work, dominated by castle and cathedral.

Everyday there is something . . . a floodlit church . . . a familiar face . . . agreeable weather . . . an unusual bird . . . a friendly wave . . . some secret thoughts . . . a kiss.

*Wednesday 19 March*
*O go your way into his gates with thanksgiving, and into his courts with praise: be thankful unto him, and speak good of his Name.*

This evening I enjoyed a spirited production of *Mrs Warren's Profession* by Bernard Shaw.

*Thursday 20 March*

This month's book is *Hard Times* by Charles Dickens.

*Friday 21 March*

Vernal equinox.

We were at the hospital gates terminus tonight (there was a pheasant and dove-cotes picture on the wall) when one old man said, 'I've lived here sixty-three years. I came here when my parents died, and I was fifteen; now I'm seventy-eight.' He said he'd been well looked after – yet I was horrified.

*Saturday 22 March*

Thou wert ever close to me
And yet I searched for Thee till the evening shadows fell.
Lalladed (Kashmir poetess)

*Sunday 23 March*

Palm Sunday.

'Standing on tiptoe for an instant in the swaying crowd, Demetrius caught a fleeting glimpse of the obvious centre of interest, a brown-haired, bareheaded, well-favoured Jew. A tight little circle had been left open for the slow advance of the shaggy white donkey on which he rode. It instantly occurred to Demetrius that this coronation project was an impromptu affair for which no preparation had been made. Certainly there had been no effort to bedeck the pretender with any royal regalia. He was clad in a simple brown mantle with no decorations of any kind, and the handful of men – his intimate friends, no doubt – who tried to shield him from the pressure of the throng wore the commonest sort of country garb . . . It was difficult to believe that this was the sort of person who could be expected to inflame a mob into some audacious action. Instead of receiving the applause with an air of triumph – or even of satisfaction – the unresponsive man on the white donkey seemed sad about the whole affair. He looked as if he would gladly have had none of it . . . The face of the enigmatic Jew seemed weighted with an almost insupportable burden of anxiety. The eyes, narrowed as if in resigned acceptance of some inevitable catastrophe, stared straight ahead toward Jerusalem. Perhaps the man, intent upon larger responsibilities far removed from this pitiable little coronation farce, wasn't really hearing the racket at all.

Now there was a temporary blocking of the way, and the noisy procession came to a complete stop. The man on the white donkey straightened, as if roused from a reverie, sighed deeply, and slowly turned his head. Demetrius watched, with parted lips and a pounding heart. The meditative eyes, drifting about over the excited multitude, seemed to carry a sort of wistful compassion for these helpless victims of an aggression for which they thought he had a remedy. Everyone was shouting, shouting – all but the Corinthian slave, whose throat was so dry he couldn't have shouted, who had no inclination to shout, who wished they would all be quiet, quiet! It wasn't the time or place for shouting. Quiet! This man wasn't the sort of person one shouted at, or shouted for. Quiet! That was what this moment called for – Quiet!

Gradually the brooding eyes moved over the crowd until they came to rest on the strained, bewildered face of Demetrius. Perhaps, he wondered, the man's gaze halted there because he alone – in all this welter of hysteria – refrained from shouting. His silence singled him out. The eyes calmly appraised Demetrius. They neither widened nor smiled; but, in some indefinable manner, they held Demetrius in a grip so firm it was almost a physical compulsion. The message they communicated was something other than sympathy, something more vital than friendly concern; a sort of stabilizing power that swept away all such negations as slavery, poverty, or any other afflicting circumstance. Demetrius was suffused with the glow of this curious kinship. Blind with sudden tears, he elbowed through the throng and reached the roadside.'[1]

I watch very little television, but I enjoyed an evening's viewing tonight. I saw the otter film *Ring of Bright Water* and – much sterner stuff – a production of *King Lear*.

*Monday 24 March*

A very tiring shift. I came home at 3.30, had my dinner, and fell asleep. Evensong during Holy Week means plainsong and Fauxbourdons, and the proper psalms.

*Lord, I have loved the habitation of thy house: and the place where thine honour dwelleth.*

[1] Lloyd C. Douglas, *The Robe*, Peter Davies 1943, pp. 70–72.

*Tuesday 25 March*

Today I completed a historical study of thirty churches, chapels, and religious houses which once existed in the quarter of old Norwich where I live. It was a mammoth task, and has taken five years. Though essentially a study in church history, it has proved much more than an abstract, academic exercise. My thinking has been stimulated, and my Christian faith stirred and enriched. But many times I nearly gave up, and the production of this thesis takes its place alongside my first two years in the ministry spent in the slums of Glasgow, and the two years I served as branch chairman, as the three most significant influences on my life over the past twelve years.

*Into thy hands I commend my spirit: for thou hast redeemed me, O Lord, thou God of truth.*

*Wednesday 26 March*

*For it is not an open enemy, that hath done me this dishonour: for then I could have borne it.*
*Neither was it mine adversary, that did magnify himself against me: for then peradventure I would have hid myself from him.*
*But it was even thou, my companion: my guide, and mine own familiar friend.*

The anthem was beautiful: 'Hear my prayer' by Purcell.

*Thursday 27 March*

Maundy Thursday. I received holy communion before going to work.

'On this day our Lord went again to Jerusalem. In the evening in the Upper Room, He washed the feet of the disciples, and instituted the blessed Sacrament of His Body and Blood. He spoke the words of comfort and peace, gave the promise of the coming of the Holy Spirit, and made the great intercession. In the Garden of Gethsemane He endured His agony. Betrayed by Judas and arrested by His enemies, He was taken to prison and to judgment.'[1]

Saviour, Thou didst the mystery give,
That I Thy nature might partake;
Thou bidd'st me outward signs receive,
One with Thyself my soul to make;

[1] *Prayers for the Christian Year*, OUP, 2nd edn. 1952, p. 96. Reprinted by permission of the Committee on Public Worship and Aids to Devotion of the General Assembly of the Church of Scotland.

My body, soul, and spirit join
Inseparably one with Thine.
Charles Wesley

*Friday 28 March*

Good Friday. Stripped altars. Hot Cross buns.

This is one day of the year I dislike having to work, but Tony and I were detailed to do a shift so I had to make the best of it. Curious weather – it snowed furiously this morning, but the afternoon was bright and dry.

Evensong – no Glorias.

*I waited patiently for the Lord: and he inclined unto me, and heard my calling.*

Beautiful anthems: O vos omnes (Gesualdo); Crus fidelis (King John of Portugal); Crucifixus (Lotti).

Crucifixion is about daring to let go. It is about daring to let go of self-sufficiency and independence, daring to love, and daring to accept the consequences. It is an awesome and frightening experience. Little wonder that we search for some other way: for an alternative path through life, less vulnerable, more secure; for an approach to each day which will leave us admired, but not exposed. For it is from this that we shrink. We long to communicate – to be liked and appreciated and understood – but we are terrified of lowering the defences. Around ourselves we erect strong fortifications – the front which people see and mistake for the *real* us, hidden beneath. And so we are protected.

But strong defences not only keep unwelcomed intruders at a safe distance; they tend, also, to imprison those who have sought sanctuary within. Nonetheless, the person is a fool who would carelessly (if not deliberately) blow a hole in that great protective facade without carefully weighing the consequences. It is comforting to be beholden to no one; but it can also be frightfully lonely. There's the rub. We are not anxious for others to have claims upon us; neither do we wish them to find out too much about us: but we *do* want relationships. For some we feel a strange and deep attraction, while a great many others evoke our interest, our sympathy, and our compassion. In short, we want to love and to be loved – in all the wide range of relationships which that small word implies. But to love is to become vulnerable. It means leaving the safety (and the isolation) of the barricade, and taking a step towards other people. And in that instant you become a sitting target. Those who love only a little can usually be hurt only a little. But those who love greatly – who are warm and open in their dealings, who do not fear what people think, who are generous in their judgments and in their deeds, who accept others for what they are – these are in great peril. Love begets love; yet sometimes it begets rejection. When people grow close in the mystery of relationship, or when acts of mercy and charity and simple kindness are performed, then love is self-authenticated; it shines in all the beauty of its brilliance and makes us certain that, in truth, it was for this we were made. But love can be a messy business. Being open and unguarded, it is possible to be wounded in a trice. A word from a person particularly dear, or an act of kindness thrown back in the face – this is all that is needed. No stray missile penetrating the old defences ever had such devastating effect.

The shock of rejection and the abuse of love: that's crucifixion.

God dared to let go of his divine self-sufficiency when, in love, he formed the creation. Christ dared to let go of the divine glory of the Father's immediate presence when, in love, he was incarnate by the Holy Ghost of the Virgin Mary. And the life of Jesus was spent in a continuous attitude of openness, acceptance, and compassion which was love incarnate. All other ways were deliberately put aside; steadfastly he set his face towards Jerusalem. Love was denied; love was betrayed; love was crucified. And love was undefeated!

How easy it is to talk glibly about the way of the cross! The cross is ugly and offensive. There are few pains more searing than the pain of rejection. Yet the church insists on preaching love. It accepts that love is often the gateway to suffering – but believes that love is worth it; believes that love may even be magnified by it. Jesus was crucified, but victorious. Love did not give way to bitterness; it endured. But crucifixion gave way: it gave way to resurrection. And this is our faith.

Fronts and barriers lead to petty and impoverished little lives. Love, friendship, companionship, and service lead to enriching relationships, beyond measure and without price. The risks are real, but so are the prizes. Rejection, misunderstanding, abuse, exploitation and ingratitude should be met with courage and with meekness and with forgiveness – not once only, but again and again. For the acceptance of the risk of crucifixion is the door to resurrection.

Be prepared for your love to be put on a cross, and you will find there is more love in the world than you had ever dreamed.



*Saturday 29 March*

Easter Even.

Our first journey today was to Shipdham, the birthplace of that famous Congregational martyr Henry Barrowe, who was hanged at Tyburn with John Greenwood on 6 April 1593. I think of him whenever I go to Shipdham. After their execution Queen Elizabeth asked the learned Dr Reynolds what he thought of these men. Reynolds was loth to speak, but being charged upon his allegiance to do so, he answered that he was persuaded 'if they had lived they would have been two as worthy instruments of the Church of God as have been raised up in this age'. Her Majesty sighed, and said no more.

This afternoon I conducted the wedding of a busman's daughter. She married a Spaniard, and his Roman Catholic parents – who understood no English – had flown to England to be present. The service was held in The Old Meeting House, and to make them feel welcome I wore a gold cope from the parish church and slipped a sentence of Latin into the rubric. Outrageous, in a Free Church? Or a simple expression of pastoral care?

I read Isaiah chapter 46 aloud in the empty church tonight, and gave thanks for this discipline which has made me look forward to Easter more eagerly than ever. At eight o'clock I attended the Holy Ceremonies and Solemn Mass of the Vigil.

*Sunday 30 March*

Easter Day. Christ is risen! He is risen indeed!

The leap from Good Friday to Easter Day is breath-taking. Solemnity becomes gaiety, black becomes gold, mourning becomes rejoicing, defeat becomes victory. Jesus lives!

Our lives display much deadness. Once we had talents, but they were never developed; once we had dreams, but they were never pursued; once we had ideals, but we let them slip away; once we had faith, but we lost it; once we could pray, but we neglected the ability; once the world sparkled like a jewel and we gazed at it with wonder, but now we have become 'scientific' and cold and matter-of-fact. So much has died. But Jesus Christ offers life and resurrection!

Or look at it this way. Once we were much more warm and kind – until we discovered that the world exploits warmth and kindness, so we became hard and selfish: and something in us died. But Jesus spoke of another kind of death – the death of self. He taught that if only we would forget our 'rights', and refuse to return evil for evil, and humbly reckon others more important than ourselves, we would pass through crucifixion and know the unspeakable joy of resurrection – the joy of those whose minds are stayed upon God and have rediscovered the secret of secrets: that living is about loving.

These are the great Easter themes – life, victory, triumph. The last word is with God and the last word is love. This love is so strong that all the enemies of human gladness cannot stand against it, even the last enemy which is death.

Concelebrated a joyful eucharist at the parish church this morning. The strange weather continues – it was snowing hard as we left church!

The children enjoyed their Easter eggs.

This afternoon was bright, dry, and cold. I attended a moving festal evensong which included the Jesus College, Cambridge Service (Mathias), Te Deum (Britten in C), and psalm 118:

*O give thanks unto the Lord, for he is gracious: because his mercy endureth for ever . . .*
*The Lord is my strength, and my song: and is become my salvation . . .*
*I shall not die, but live: and declare the works of the Lord.*
*The Lord hath chastened and corrected me: but he hath not given me over unto death . . .*
*The same stone which the builders refused: is become the head-stone in the corner.*
*This is the Lord's doing: and it is marvellous in our eyes.*
*This is the day which the Lord hath made: we will rejoice and be glad in it.*

*Monday 31 March*

The special joy of Easter Day last longer than the excitement of Christmas Day. It was still Easter this morning, and I attended eight o'clock holy communion:

'Almighty God, who through thy only-begotten Son Jesus Christ hast overcome death, and opened unto us the gate of everlasting life; We humbly beseech thee, that, as by thy special grace preventing us thou dost put into our minds good desires, so by thy continual help we may bring the same to good effect; through Jesus Christ our Lord, who liveth and reigneth with thee and the Holy Ghost, ever one God, world without end. Amen.' 

This is the obituary day of the third of my personal heroes – John Donne, poet and preacher. Donne was born in London in 1573; he died on 31 March 1631, having spent the last years of his life as Dean of St Paul's and the most illustrious preacher of his day.

John Donne is the greatest of the English love-poets. Among the *Elegies* my favourite is 'To his Mistris Going to Bed', which George Saintsbury described as 'a piece of frank naturalism, redeemed from coarseness by passion and poetic completeness':

Licence my roving hands, and let them goe
Behind, before, above, between, below.
Oh my America, my new found lande,
My kingdome, safeliest when with one man man'd,
My myne of precious stones, my Empiree,
How blest am I in this discovering thee.
To enter in these bonds is to be free,
Then where my hand is set my seal shall be.
Full nakedness, all joyes are due to thee.
As soules unbodied, bodies uncloth'd must bee
To taste whole joyes . . .
Then since I may knowe,
As liberally as to a midwife showe
Thy selfe; cast all, yea this white linnen hence.
Here is no pennance, much lesse innocence.
To teach thee, I am naked first: Why than
What need'st thou have more covering than a man.

The situations dramatized in the *Songs and Sonnets* vary widely (and if space permitted I would quote pages of examples!). I like 'The Sunne Rising':

Busie old foole, unruly Sunne,
Why dost thou thus,
Through windowes, and through curtaines call on us?
Must to thy motions lovers seasons run?
Sawcy pedantique wretch, goe chide
Late schoole boyes, and sowre prentices,
Goe tell Court-huntsmen, that the King will ride,

Call countrey ants to harvest offices;
Love, all alike, no season knowes, nor clyme,
Nor houres, dayes, months, which are the rags of time.

Like his master Ovid, who in this stands apart from the tradition of classical love-poetry, Donne appears wholly uninterested in homosexual love, though his *Verse Letters* show that his friendships were particularly important to him. To Mr I. L. went the primacy of honour and affection:

Of that short Roll of friends writ in my heart
Which with thy name begins . . .

John Donne's *Divine Poems* are full of the rare spiritual insight which characterize his sermons. One of the most famous is 'A Hymne to God the Father':

Wilt thou forgive that sinne where I begunne,
Which is my sin, though it were done before?
Wilt thou forgive those sinnes through which I runne,
And doe them still; though still I doe deplore?
When thou hast done, thou hast not done,
For, I have more.

Wilt thou forgive that sinne by which I wonne
Others to sinne? and, made my sinne their doore?
Wilt thou forgive that sinne which I did shunne
A yeare, or two: but wallowed in, a score?
When thou hast done, thou hast not done,
For, I have more.

I have a sinne of feare, that when I have spunne
My last thred, I shall perish on the shore;
Sweare by thy selfe, that at my death thy Sunne
Shall shine as it shines now, and heretofore;
And, having done that, Thou hast done,
I have no more.

Donne's best-known sermon – on the mercy of God – was preached from Isaiah 7.14 in St Paul's on the evening of Christmas Day, 1624:

'He brought light out of darknesse, not out of a lesser light; he can bring thy Summer out of Winter, though thou have no Spring; though in the wayes of fortune, or understanding, or conscience, thou have been benighted till now, wintred and frozen, clouded and eclypsed, damped and benummed, smothered and stupified till now, now God comes to thee, not as in the dawning of the day, not as in the bud of the spring, but as the Sun at noon to illustrate all shadowes, as the sheaves in harvest, to fill all penuries, all occasions invite his mercies, and all times are his seasons.'

What preacher of the gospel would not give everything to be able to preach like that?

The popular distinction between 'Jack Donne' and 'Doctor Donne' was first made by Donne himself. Helen Gardner comments: 'It is often used to distinguish Donne the satirist and amorous poet from Donne the religious poet and preacher, "Jack" being licentious and the "Doctor" grave and moral. Donne himself was distinguishing between himself as a young man writing as an individual, and himself as an older man in orders, writing with the authority and the responsibility that a profession gives and demands. In one sense, all his poetry, whether amorous or religious, licentious or moral, was the work of "Jack Donne".'[1]

It is those depths of sensuality and spirituality combined in the one person which comprise the secret of John Donne's fascination for me. The Lothian Portrait captures the amorous Donne, with sensuous lips and fingers ready to rove 'behind, before, above, between, below'. Donne, the preacher and divine, is held most perfectly in the words (uttered with a reluctant eye upon the hourglass) with which he concluded a sermon on I Thessalonians 5.16: 'It is time to end: but as long as the glasse hath a gaspe, as long as I have one, I would breathe in this ayre, in this perfume, in this breath of heaven, the contemplation of this Joy.'

*Tuesday 1 April*

Instead of taking Molly a second cup of tea in bed early this morning I took a cup of warm water, for an April Fool. In the darkness she began to drink it, and I hurried from the room. When the cry of indignation failed to arrive, I returned to the bedroom puzzled and suspicious. The cup stood on the floor, nearly empty! 'I've only left a mouthful,' she said. 'I think you forgot to put in any sugar, dear, but I didn't want to complain.'

Crestfallen and crushed, I tried no more April Fools today!

On the way to work I saw a grey wagtail beside the river.

[1] In her introduction to *The Elegies, Songs and Sonnets of John Donne*, OUP 1965, pp. xviiif.

*Wednesday 2 April*
The first clumps of king-cups were gleaming in a marshy field this afternoon. They are among my favourite flowers; I associate them with expeditions to collect frog-spawn, newts, and tadpoles, when I wore short trousers.

*Thursday 3 April*
In the bus, we passed a camera shop which offered what was termed an 'Exposure Service'. Tony was quite overcome.

Frequent April showers – though not of rain, but of hail.

Today I was filled yet again with an overwhelming realization of my true richness. These must be the best years, to which I shall look back with thankfulness. I am just old enough to have had a little experience of life, but young enough to be close to the generation beneath me; I enjoy my work; the children are growing fast, and make the house a place of noise and bustling activity; I still have plenty of energy. Each day (as I must already have said) seems like a gift.

*Friday 4 April*
I don't know if ultimate reality is personal; or, to put it in everyday language – I don't know if God exists. I hope he does, and I work on the assumption that he does. Others, apparently, hope he doesn't, or can't even accept the possibility that he may – and they base their lives on the assumption that he doesn't. Neither can prove or demonstrate that the other is wrong.

My personal hopes and beliefs vary from day to day. On some days I believe much more than I do on others. But even on the bad days I still cling to my assumption; I try to live as in the sight of God. This weakness of insight, and these everlasting doubts, do not vitally affect my preaching. The task of the preacher is not to air his personal views, but to proclaim the faith of the church.

I do not believe it is irrational to set great store upon a faith which is incapable of scientific demonstration. Many of the most precious things in human experience – like loyalty, and friendship – seem equally to defy scientific analysis, and appeal instead to a 'higher', intuitive law.

To accept the existence of God as a working hypothesis is to possess at least one satisfying point of reference from which to contemplate the phenomenon of human existence. God set the creative process into motion; God upholds the entire creation instant by instant; God is the designer of a myriad different forms which are in perfect interrelation; God is the giver of life. To posit God as the agent (possessing 'personality') responsible for these basic facts of being is no less convincing than to ascribe the relevant processes to nameless, abstract, scientific forces. On the contrary, the idea of God seems far more appealing, and rings far more true (for me).

But I cannot prove God exists. Nor can anybody else. Those who claim a direct knowledge don't convince me of much. Perhaps they're lucky; I only wish more would give greater evidence of that knowledge in their bearing.

There are some things, however, in which I believe utterly. I believe in the church. I believe its history can be traced back two thousand years to Jesus of Nazareth, of whose own historicity I can entertain no serious doubts.

I believe that the gospels – despite all the problems of New Testament criticism – provide a clear and consistent account of the life of Jesus. I find a unique quality of attractiveness and authority in that picture. The attitudes Jesus adopts and advocates strike true, and I feel (indeed, I *know*) I ought to be like that.

I am aware of an immense gulf between my actions and attitudes, and those displayed by Jesus of Nazareth in the gospels.

I believe that love – New Testament agape – is the key, the secret, of human fulfilment.

I believe love is regularly crucified, but that resurrection can follow crucifixion.

I believe there is an immense and powerful potency in the Christian tradition – in the prayers, scriptures, worship, hymns, fellowship, and eucharist – which is strong and contagious; mix with these people, participate in these things, and the agape displayed by Jesus will begin to grow in you. All depends upon how greatly you desire the gift. Those who seek little find little; those who long for more find the supply is endless. Without violence being done either to free will or personality, I believe there is strength, joy, peace, and love to be caught in practising Christianity. Egocentricity is lessened, personality is enhanced, new poise and integrity appear, new dimensions of character are born. In short, we become gradually a little more like Jesus. And though we can prove nothing, the idea of God becomes more credible, more real.

I can't understand the mechanics of these things. Not today, anyhow. These thoughts have come to me during a hard shift. Tomorrow, perhaps, I may write in a totally different vein, and be much more sure about many more things; but I don't feel like that today. I know nothing. Faith seems almost a nonsense. But I will cling to it for another day. Though I cannot show you God, the things I have told you I *do* believe I believe with all my heart. 

*Saturday 5 April*

'I don't want my life to obey any other will but my own' – Simone de Beauvoir, at the age of nineteen.

*Sunday 6 April*

The violence we have done to our consciences and to our intuitions must be righted by an act of cosmic forgiveness. Only thus can we be brought into harmony with the whole created order. For sin is not a private affair involving a few actions of doubtful morality. Sin is the refusal – sometimes deliberate, sometimes involuntary – to be actuated by love. And since the entire universe is fired by love, sin cannot be other than cosmic in its scope and implications. Sin is alienation; sin is estrangement. Sin destroys our peace (our inner unity), and separates us from each other. To sin is to become divorced from the scent of the pine woods, the cry of the redshank, the rise and fall of the tides. Divine forgiveness, therefore, is not a purely personal matter, but an act which involves the moon and stars.

*Monday 7 April*

Time is a cheat who regulates his ways
According to the wishes of my heart;
With spiteful mirth, he touches empty days
And turns to years the hours that we're apart.
Alone, I try to visualize your face
And catch the graceful beauty of your form;
I long for Time to skip with careless pace,
To bring you near, and calm this madd'ning storm.
But Time demurs until, At last! we meet –
And then his evil work begins again:
The precious moments speed on eager feet,
And my attempts to hold them fast are vain.
I do not plead for Time to be more fair
But cheat on my behalf, when you are here.

*Tuesday 8 April*

Our thrush continues to dominate the swelling dawn chorus, but he has been joined by other voices.

*Yea, even mine own familiar friend, whom I trusted: who did also eat of my bread, hath laid great wait for me.*

The seasons seem to be running about two months late: tonight it is snowing, and the flakes caught in the church floodlights have a hypnotic effect.

*Wednesday 9 April*

Several interesting and 'worthwhile' conversations occurred at work.

Choral evensong was broadcast from the cathedral. I was on duty and couldn't attend – but fortunately I was able to hear most of the service on the radio in the canteen. I didn't turn it up too loud, and stood with my ear close to the set while a card-school continued in session beside me.

This evening I saw a pair of long-tailed tits in the ailanthus tree – the first occasion I have recorded this species in the city centre.

*Thursday 10 April*

This month's book – *Watership Down* by Richard Adams – I found absorbing and enchanting.

Sorting through some old letters, I was amused to read one I received at Christmas two years ago. The writer had been to a Christmas gathering for worship at a Friends' Meeting, and had been surprised and delighted to see a small girl allowed to light a special Christmas candle. He commented: 'Throw Catholicism out of the front door and it will creep in again through the back!' I'm sure that's true.

*Friday 11 April*

I attended a service of thanksgiving for the restoration of the cathedral – a joyful occasion celebrated in the presence of Her Majesty the Queen. The service was simple yet impressive – the Church of England at its best. The specially-composed 'Fanfare for Her Majesty' – in which the trumpeters of the Household Cavalry, in uniforms of gold, combined with the choir to greet the Queen – was an exciting and worthy opening to an act of worship which marked the culmination of twenty-five years of major work on the cathedral church.

I returned home to learn that a much-loved neighbour had died suddenly.

Of such contrasting events is the fabric of our existence. Joy and celebration overlap with suffering and bereavement.

*Saturday 12 April*

Things have changed a good deal since D. H. Lawrence felt it necessary to write: 'Whoever the God was that made us, he made us complete. He didn't stop at the navel and leave the rest to the devil. It is too childish . . .' Nonetheless, Christians continue to make astonishingly heavy weather of the facts of sexuality. We are far quicker to make moral and ethical evaluations than we are to recognize and accept the facts – when the former should be based upon the latter! The basic truth Christians find most difficult to assimilate concerns the diversity and complexity of human sexuality. We seem incapable of recognizing the existence of every conceivable gradation of temperament between exclusive heterosexuality and exclusive homosexuality, comparable to the wide political spectrum within a parliament. No grounds exist for turning this elementary fact into high drama. Imagine a law by which left-footed people were precluded from playing football, or a regulation which insisted that those who can kick with either foot must decide between one or the other. How the game would be impoverished!

It is at this point only that the Christian ethicist may properly commence his observations: these, however, are usually so vague and half-baked that nobody bothers to listen. Marriage or vivid nocturnal phantasies – logically, those are the Christian alternatives (and even that option is phoney, for traditionally Christians have prayed to be delivered from evil thoughts and phantoms of the night, so the one crude choice collapses through lack of realism). The harmless and immense pleasure of masturbation (and its importance in providing release from unbearable tension) is seldom stressed in Christian literature. The outstanding feature of the sexually active individual (certainly among males) is the marked need for variety. No comment. Christian study-groups diagnose sexual boredom and staleness as an important contributory factor in the breakdown of many marriages – but there the defence rests. Modern women are able to choose to use their sex for fun or for love; if for love, then either with or without marriage, and with or without children. These new choices and this new freedom raise questions about human relationships which make Christians distinctly uneasy. 

The fact of heterosexuality is regarded, apparently, by many Christians as the act of a God who ought to have known better – though, secretly, they would agree with the boys at work who assert openly that if he made anything better he kept it for himself.

But if good, 'natural' heterosexuality presents problems of embarrassing perplexity, these pale to insignificance beside the horrific facts of homosexuality and bisexuality. Christians, in common with many others, prefer not to think about these things at all. Maybe it is as well, for most of their observations have tended either to be wildly inaccurate or grossly unchristian. 'Judge not, that ye be not judged . . .' Ye gods!

Human beings are fascinating in their variety, and are to be enjoyed – not hurt, not abused, not exploited – but enjoyed. We have no greater say in the sexuality we inherit than in selecting the colour of our eyes – and no greater degrees of virtue or blame are involved. But what we do with the material we have been given depends upon our philosophy and our responsibility.

*Sunday 13 April*

The sticky buds on the horse-chestnut trees are unfolding; I peer, and feel a sense of reverence.

*Monday 14 April*

Tony was full of wit today, both deliberate and unintentional. He declared that hairy legs are a sign of gorillity, and then produced a spoonerism: 'I gave him a hair-bug' – meaning, 'I gave him a bear-hug'.

*Tuesday 15 April*

A letter in *The Times* today from the Reverend Mervyn Wilson earned my warm approval. An earlier letter from the Carlisle diocese had visualized the priest of the future offering 'specialized and professional services of leadership and guidance, high standards spiritual and intellectual, as upheld by frequent intervals of advanced training'. Mervyn Wilson replied:

'Will there be no room for some to take another way? Here, I might be a park keeper in the old churchyard: easy to find, with time to study and write. There the modern pastor could tend his flock. Or a priest might be a window-cleaner or petrol-pump attendant. His chosen job should be (a) below his capacity (b) leave his heart free and mind uncluttered. There is a charm in this and a good gospel challenge to the world's values.'

*Wednesday 16 April*
Flesh. The soft, 'more than vellum warmth' of youth (William Golding). The cold, sunken, crinkled skin of the old man found dead in his chair this morning.

*Thursday 17 April*
This morning, on a country route, from the cab I noticed: a goldfinch; plenty of flowering gorse; a spring-crazy lapwing; a solid bank of purple honesty; a great elm, with every bud splitting open. New life is surging out of the earth.

*Friday 18 April*
The warm weather has brought out the summer blouses and dresses.

*Saturday 19 April*
I conducted a funeral, then worked a late shift.

I found myself thinking about faith, hope, and charity – and their secular equivalents. We have *knowledge* of facts and phenomena, in which we are prepared to *believe*. Our belief results in *rational action*. The secular formula, therefore, is *belief*, *knowledge*, *rational action*. Alongside this exists a sacred formula; we attach different labels to our religious categories, but the attitudes and processes involved are not dissimilar. We have a glorious Christian *hope*, upon which we have learned to rely, in *faith*. Our faith issues in *charity* (love) – which is super-rational. The sacred formula for interpreting human experience, therefore, is *faith*, *hope*, *charity*.

*Sunday 20 April*
The 'Old Meeting Church Booke' is a fascinating volume over which I have pored many hours. It recounts the founding of the church in the stormy days of the seventeenth century, and often the entries are moving in their simplicity and sincerity. Some entries, however, have gained a quaintness over the centuries, and it is impossible to suppress a smile as one reads them. In May 1650, for example, worldly influences proved too strong for two young women members of the church, Elizabeth Thurstone and Elizabeth

Townsend. Both were summoned to appear before the church, and the case against Elizabeth Townsend is recorded as follows: 

'16 May 1650. After the Church out of tendernes had waited some tyme & sent divers times messengers to Elizabeth Townsend to appeare before the Church to give satisfaction for the scandalls following proved against her as followeth:

1. That the said Elizabeth Townsend hath divers tymes forsaken the Church-assemblyes upon the Lords dayes & spent the tyme with Dan Beck, Samuel Puckle & other very scandalous persons in vaine foolish & prophane discourse . . .

2. That after shee was solemnely admonished not to keepe company with such prophane & scandalous persons, yet she mett with the saide company on the Lords day, & heard them read out of a booke called the flying rowle, which occasioned much foolish laughter among them; which booke also (being full of cursed swearing & horrid blasphemies) she borrowed & caryed away with her . . .

6. That shee with another went together to the house of one Balles (who is accounted a wizard) to enquire of him concerning a young mans taking a maide to be his wife, which thing she being charged with as a greate evill & very offensive to many, she excused it by an untrueth, falsly charging one of the Church to encourage her to doe soe . . .'

On this occasion Elizabeth was admonished by the Pastor, but to no good effect. A fortnight later, the following entry was made in the book:

'30 May 1650. Upon the sad experience of the disorderly walking of Elizabeth Townsend, her continuance therein, & her lying impenitent under admonition, and her refusing to heare the Church, The Pastor with consent of the Church declared her to be unfitt for Communion and (as one that walked disorderly & stubbornly) to be withdrawne from by the Church in all the ordinances of communion, & messengers were appointed to declare the same unto her.'

*Monday 21 April*

Frank – friend, philosopher, and high churchman – sent me a note:

'Catholic Christianity portrays us living in an essentially dramatic universe, where time and again the fate of the cosmos depends upon all-significant confrontations. What happens when the serpent tempts Eve? What will come about when Gabriel visits the house of Mary? How will our Lord reply when the devil tempts him in the wilderness? What will the two Marys see in the garden? All epitomized, of course, in the drama of the Mass.'

*Tuesday 22 April*

The fresh green of hawthorn and larch; the new leaves on the horse chestnut hanging like the wings of a freshly-emerged hawk-moth, waiting for strength to flow into them; daffodils, which have had a long season this year; the scent of yellow wallflowers drifting into the cab as I sped past a flower-bed in the city; comfrey.

*Wednesday 23 April*

The feast of St George, patron saint of England. I worked an early shift, then conducted a funeral.

*Tremble, thou earth, at the presence of the Lord: at the presence of the God of Jacob;*
*Who turned the hard rock into a standing water: and the flint-stone into a springing well.*

This evening I went to the theatre and saw *The Tempest.*

*Thursday 24 April*

*My soul melteth away for very heaviness: comfort thou me according unto thy word.*

When a programme of which Granny suspects she may disapprove appears on television, she doesn't turn her attention elsewhere or have an early night – she watches avidly, and disapproves at great length.

*Friday 25 April*

A heavy dew sparkled on the fields and hedges early this morning, but by eight o'clock the sky was dull and overcast. There are rewards for early rising.

*O how sweet are thy words unto my throat: yea, sweeter than honey unto my mouth.*

I listened, tonight, to a blackbird; the song is more rich and melodious, and less repetitive than the song-thrush.

*Saturday 26 April*
Great excitement! Despite all fears, Norwich City has won promotion to the First Division.

*Sunday 27 April*
This morning I preached at the eucharist, conducted a short memorial service, and interred some ashes. I had to work this afternoon, but I didn't mind – it was one of those rare occasions on which the two chief spheres of my existence moved into conjunction. I drove the cathedral choir to sing evensong at Swaffham! Yes, I was actually paid time-and-a-half to listen to choral evensong! Perhaps I have the best of all worlds, after all! Arriving back in The Close I was surprised to notice that the illuminated spire of the cathedral seemed to throw a shadow on the clouds. I saw a parable in that. The events of this world cast a shadow upon heaven, and have eternal significance.

*Monday 28 April*
*I will worship toward thy holy temple, and praise thy Name, because of thy loving-kindness and truth: for thou hast magnified thy Name, and thy Word, above all things.*

Today was the twentieth anniversary of my conversion, as a boy of fifteen, to the Christian faith. I was sent to Sunday school as a child, hated it, and left as soon as possible. Yet as I moved into adolescence I seem to have possessed a kind of natural religion, which had nothing to do with chapel Sunday school. It may have been born in the day-school Bible stories from infant and junior schools, but it came to be linked far more closely to my interest in natural history, and my sense of wonder at the creation.

I have preserved my nature diary for 1954, written when I was aged fourteen. It contains good sketches of alder and willow catkins, and accounts of incidents which would still provoke similar responses: the excitement of seeing a green woodpecker picking insects off the flowers on a grave; my revulsion and horror at the sight of myxomatosis; the return of the sand-martins on 20 May; 'the splendour of the silver spell which the full moon cast upon everything'; owls and bats.

There are also two or three more specifically religious entries. Easter Day, for example, is marked with the text: 'But they constrained him, saying, Abide with us: for it is toward evening, and the day is far spent.' There is a curious entry in my ordinary diary for that same year: 'Monday 15 March 1954 . . . All my luck is bad – going to church Sunday . . .' I kept that resolution and went to church for several Sundays – though it is not recorded whether or not my luck changed!

It was the following year, however, that vague superstition became fervent commitment. On Sunday 3 April 1955 (which was Palm Sunday), I made one of my occasional visits to the Methodist church whose Sunday school I had abhorred. A note in my diary records the event: 'After the morning service, I was caught on the steps of the church by the vicar, who invited me to the weekly functions. I guardedly accepted.' The minister, John Sharp, introduced me to some of the young people at the church – an ordeal I found acutely embarrassing – and I began, that week, to attend the youth club and Christian Endeavour.

The next important event occurred two weeks later: 'Monday 18 April – Went to hear a Billy Graham relay service from Kelvin Hall, Glasgow, at Silver Road Baptist Church. I resisted going forward at the end, but against myself.' That evening was vital. For the first time in my life the Christian religion had made a personal impact on me, and I was shaken. I had had no idea that Christianity demanded a verdict. I can remember walking home, disconsolately kicking a screwed-up fish-and-chip paper which had been thrown on the pavement, unhappy because I felt I should have said 'Yes' to God and had not been strong enough.

Ten days afterwards I went to another relay service with other young people from the church; when the appeal was made to accept Christ, I went forward to signify my decision and my desire to become a Christian: 'Thursday 28 April – Heard another Billy Graham relay from Glasgow at Chapel Field Road Methodist Church. This time I could not resist the call. Truly a great day.

Blessed assurance, Jesus is mine:
O what a foretaste of glory divine!'

That is the event which, with inexpressible gratitude, I am celebrating today. That is the way in which God reached out to me. What adolescent emotional drives were at work I leave others skilled in those matters to divine. I am not ashamed at the simplicity of this account; I have not cheated – I have quoted the original documents! Those are the facts, as I recall them – the Christian message suddenly became meaningful, and I wanted to be a follower of Christ's teaching and a member of the church. I wanted God's forgiveness and God's power: and I believed they had been given me. And that evening has proved the predominant influence in my life throughout the twenty years which have followed, overshadowing all other influences and events, and bringing me to this time and place, rejoicing. 

*Tuesday 29 April*

I revelled in the new green of the beech wood, clean and fresh and beautiful. It doesn't seem many days since last year's autumn-tinted leaves were being driven before the strong wind. But now brilliant spring colours are everywhere: wallflowers, tulips, polyanthus, auriculas (one of my favourites), purple iris, flowering cherry, forget-me-nots. How is it possible not to notice, and not to respond to this new life flooding through all things?

I received a postcard from one of my former conductors who married a Norwegian girl and lives now in Norway. Part of the message read: '. . . By the way, they are looking for good bus drivers here. (Never mind, they might want some bad ones.) Love Anne & Frank.'

*Wednesday 30 April*

Bluebells – primroses – a rainbow.

At the football match this evening a blackbird flew down at half-time, hunting for worms, and remained on the pitch even when the players trooped out for the second half. With a brood to feed, every hour of daylight is precious.

*Thursday 1 May*

May Day.

'What is a saint? A saint is someone who has achieved a remote human possibility. It is impossible to say what that possibility is. I think it has something to do with the energy of love. Contact with this energy results in the exercise of a kind of balance in the chaos of existence. A saint does not dissolve the chaos; if he did the world would have changed long ago. I do not think that a saint dissolves the chaos even for himself, for there is something arrogant and warlike in the notion of a man setting the universe in order. It is a kind of balance that is his glory. He rides the drifts like an escaped ski. His course is a caress of the hill. His track is a drawing of the snow in a moment of its particular arrangement with wind and rock. Something in him so loves the world that he gives himself to the laws of gravity and chance. Far from flying with the angels, he traces with the fidelity of a seismograph needle the state of the solid bloody landscape. His house is dangerous and finite, but he is at home in the world. He can love the shapes of human beings, the fine and twisted shapes of the heart. It is good to have among us such men, such balancing monsters of love. It makes me think that the numbers in the bag actually correspond to the numbers on the raffles we have bought so dearly, and so the prize is not an illusion.'[1]

*Friday 2 May*

It is time we differentiated more sharply between 'worship' and 'fellowship'. The two, of course, are closely linked. It is poor worship that does not engender a deeper sense of fellowship and mutual love among the worshippers, while the fellowship of Christian believers – assembled for prayer, study, or even social and recreational purposes – produces frequently an attitude of worship and devotion more vital than anything experienced in formal services. Yet I maintain that for practical reasons the two concepts should be separated.

Acts of worship, performed in church, are set-piece activities, the 'togetherness' of the people taking second place to the awareness of God's awful 'otherness'. To this awareness we respond by offering our highest expressions of worship. It is a formal and deliberate attempt to apprehend God's holiness and reply in the same holy and loving spirit. For me, at least, worship is not an occasion for 'folksiness' or unseemly heartiness or extreme informality. It is a solemn, sobering activity – the loftiest activity upon which I attempt to engage. In it I am assisted by forms and expressions which – in other areas of life – would quickly be dismissed as archaic. But worship is not just one activity among others. It is supreme activity. It is creature man reaching out towards God his maker. Worship should not be made deliberately cold, lifeless and obscure. These are not the synonyms of holy devotion. But warmth and simplicity should be combined with such dignity and reverence as befits creature man at his worthiest and best. I am not convinced that modern liturgical developments are achieving this balance. Many changes

[1] Leonard Cohen, *Beautiful Losers*, Jonathan Cape 1970, pp. 95f.

seem to be the work of restless clergy, who busy themselves altering things chiefly to justify their existence. In a recent sermon, an eminent cleric told his congregation they could be assured that their clergy were alert to the need for change. Don't we know it! Liturgical change is too easy. Of all the challenges confronting the modern church, liturgical alterations are often the least urgent. For what happens? The liturgy is chopped about, the ungodly are not converted, and the faithful are confused and hurt. On the rare occasions that non-churchmen attend a service, they look for an old-fashioned dignity in the words, and expect to encounter a mysterious sense of 'otherness' in the worship. They do not expect to feel that they are at just-another-meeting. To say these things is not to oppose all new suggestions. I want simply to check our perspective, and our priorities. There are far more searching and far more costly matters awaiting clerical attention than this perpetual tampering with the services. (The parson was delighted with his Series II infant baptism. But the bus driver was less impressed: '... Then he gave me a bloody candle to hold; I felt a right –'). In Bible study groups it is excellent for different versions to be used and compared: but I believe that to drop the Authorized Version from worship is madness. In a prayer-meeting, let God be addressed in whatever simple language comes naturally to the believer: but in worship I find that 'thee' (and not 'you') heightens my awareness of taking part in something which is essentially different. All these thoughts flow from the fact that I attended a Series III holy communion recently, and in addition, have just realized that after fifteen years I am heartily sick of the New English Bible. It is not, of course, that I think it less 'inspired'; it is doubtless a scholarly and much more accurate translation. But the incomparable English of the Authorized Version is in itself an aid to worship, and more than compensates for its disadvantages. I had to read Isaiah 55 in the New English Bible recently, and knew I had sold my birthright for a mess of pottage; I listened to Isaiah 40, which ought to build relentlessly up to that glorious thirty-first verse, and it fizzled out like a damp squib. In the New Testament, the Beatitudes have been de-fused: 'How blest are those who hunger and thirst to see right prevail ...' The crunch came finally the other week when I heard the gospel read at the feast of the Annunciation on Lady Day. I waited to hear: 'Hail, thou that art highly favoured, the Lord is with thee; blessed art thou among women.' Instead (to my astonishment) I heard: 

'Greetings, most favoured one! The Lord is with you.' Why not have 'Wotcha, Mary'? My unusual ministry has been costly and full-blooded. To the surprise of some of my friends, I am not very sympathetic towards what I consider gimmicky and anaemic changes for the sake of change. We want to raise people in worship. We do not serve them best by reducing worship to the level of a committee-meeting, and insisting upon the language of the market place.

*Saturday 3 May*

Spent the day on a long country walk with a friend. To retain relative sanity I need one day like this each week, but life isn't that simple. Impressions: a blustery day, with sunshine chasing light showers; the stillness of an Early English country church (with an almost tangible silence, which exists unchanged whether I am here or caught up in the city traffic ten miles away); boys playing darts in the village pub Saturday lunch time, the week's work done; theological discussion and intimate conversation along the lanes; a baby rabbit with an injured leg.

*Sunday 4 May*

A school-teacher told me of a child in her class who inquired this week during a lesson: 'If the Battle of Hastings started at 1066, what time did it finish?'

Naughty Linda secretly sketched me during the sermon this morning. It was not a flattering portrait.

A conductor attended morning worship, and I baptized the daughter of another conductor this afternoon.

*Monday 5 May*

I happened on one of the frequent do-you-remember? sessions in the canteen this morning, and heard yet again two of the standard funny stories connected with our garage.

A driver was cut-up by a mini, which had then to stop at some traffic-lights. Incensed, the bus driver climbed from his cab to remonstrate with the driver of the car. He grabbed the door-handle of the mini, but the apprehensive driver had the presence of mind to lock it. As the bus-driver gave the door-handle a terrific wrench, the traffic-lights changed, and the mini sped away leaving a thwarted bus-driver clutching a door-handle!

A woman boarded a double-decker bus which had a front en-

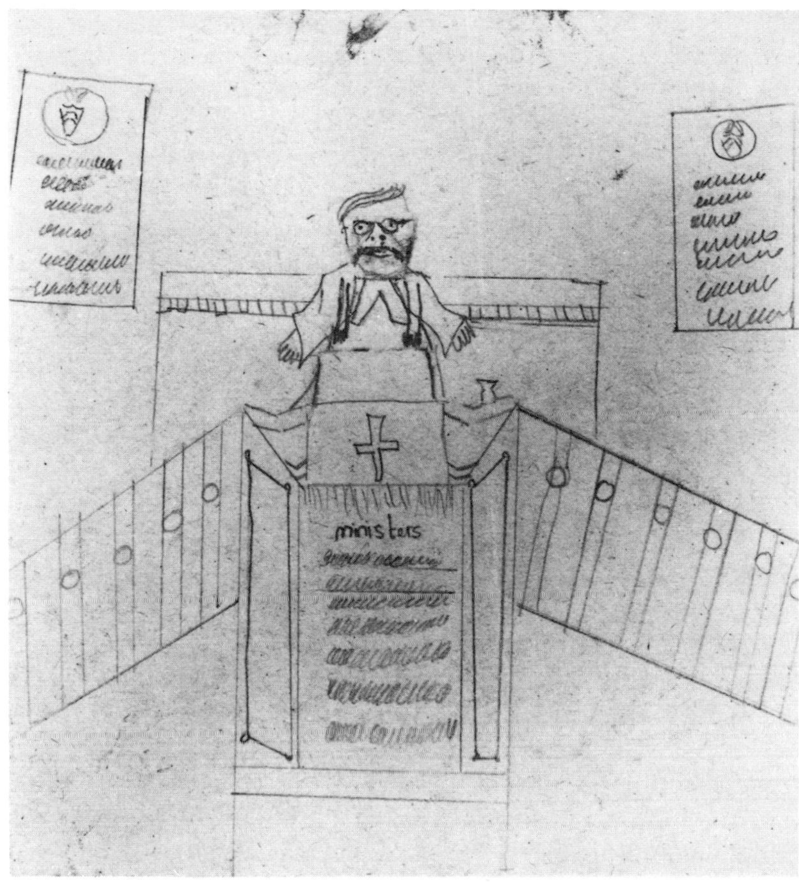


trance and doors controlled by the driver. Her small dog, fastened to a lead, remained standing on the pavement. The conductor, seeing the woman safely on the bus (but not noticing the lead), duly rang the bell. The driver closed the doors, and the bus roared away up the road with the woman screaming on the platform, clutching a lead which passed through the closed doors to the dog, which chased along the street (beside the bus) as it had never chased before! Happily, the bus stopped before serious harm was done.

There are hundreds more stories where those came from, and they lose nothing in the telling.

*Tuesday 6 May*

The two most important things in the world are religion and sex. When I say religion, I am using the word in its widest possible sense to include not only a formal religious commitment and the performance of prescribed observances, but every expression of wonder, awe, reverence and mystery. And when I say sex, I am referring to the whole spectrum of tender human relationships, of which an infinite variety can co-exist but which seem all to flow from this one fountain-head.

Those who have become so materialistic in their outlook that nothing arrests them and causes them to marvel have become dehumanized, and merit our pity. They are neither super-sophisticated nor excessively simple-minded. Persons of great intellect are usually aware, above all, of their comparative ignorance and smallness; while the man of true simplicity never ceases (like a child) to marvel. It is that erosion of values we call materialism, affecting high and low alike, which has produced the modern scarcity of true religion. The substitute idols are too pitiable to pillory: sport, cars, cheap sex, wealth. Man needs religion. The inexplicable mystery of his fleeting existence demands it. When wonder dies in a man, that which made him most truly human has vanished.

Sex is the mysterious attraction of beauty between two persons, and is linked closely with religion. There are many kinds of beauty, and many types of relationship. But all love, all warmth, all friendship, all vital companionship, all 'togetherness' is essentially sexual. Perhaps skeletons lie happily in isolation, but while they are clothed in living flesh and animated by living spirits those bodies will crave communion. People need people. For reasons more profound than mere procreation, we need to be in meaningful and loving relationship. Nothing matters more than religion and sex.

My religion finds its ordered expression in Christianity, with its great cosmic themes of creation, atonement, life and death and resurrection. From these I derive immense inspiration and comfort. My religious awareness becomes concentrated, and is channelled into a valuable and coherent entity. Christ becomes the focus of devotion. But one thing leaves me uneasy: Christianity glibly pretends (or so it seems) to have all the answers. It can produce a dogma for every occasion, and because it has everything cut and dried and labelled, it tends – paradoxically – to reduce or destroy the mystery.

Nonconformity has been particularly guilty, though by no means alone in culpability. So – latin is out, ceremonies other than the simplest rituals are unnecessary, the hymns and prayers must all be such as everyone can understand. God, apparently, is never sensed or perceived; He must be thought out. And when it comes to sex, the church is frighteningly (if unconvincingly) clear-cut in its teachings. But I'm not sure I want everything clear-cut. This is not because I am deliberately perverse, but because my experience of life is not clear-cut.

However, I embrace and revel in all the great themes and doctrines. I cling to them eagerly and devoutly – yet with a certain lightness of touch. Christ is not merely the focus of faith; he is the centre of life. But Christ has not tamed me. My cosmos has not needed to be reduced in size to accommodate him. My God is not small. He is consuming fire and unapproachable light, and though I love him with a fearful, ultimate love, I am still wild and pagan. Because I have not tried to reduce his stature, he has not reduced mine. Instead, he has inflamed me with his love – that irresistable and uncontrollable influence which bloweth where it listeth. And now I see love in the strength of the wind; I see love in the pull of the tides and the rhythm of the waves; love in the flowers; love in all the creatures; love in companionship; love in all warm meeting. There are only two great themes, and they are interwoven. The first is religion; the second is sex.

*Wednesday 7 May*

I attended synod. At lunch, I sat with a ministerial friend who was compelled to superannuate early through ill-health, but who works now at his original profession. I was interested to hear him remark how strangely satisfying it was to feel that the wages he received had been earned by the labour of his own hands. I felt exactly the same when I received my first pay-packet for bus-driving in 1968. (There is a cold anonymity about the quarterly ministerial cheque – especially when one is aware that the sum has been scraped together only with much effort.)

As I sat in synod it occurred to me that the church in England could be brought quickly to convulsions of new vitality if three matters received close, costly, and daring attention:

(a) If *unity* was recognized as an urgent priority, and Free Church ministers would accept episcopal re-ordination as an extension of their existing ministry, for the sake of the gospel.

(b) If the principle of *tithing* was re-examined and commended to the faithful.

(c) If a more *flexible ministry* could be envisaged, such as would make my present ministry appear unremarkable.

There is so little courageous realism. We are either so damned complacent that we quibble about orders (clerical status, God forgive us) and other peripheral matters while the ship goes down – or we dash away in a panic reaction and alter all the wrong things (which, by a happy coincidence, we can do without causing ourselves much pain). We chop the services about; Salvation Army girls abandon the bonnet which is universally recognized and respected, and exchange it for a new and anonymous device; 'trendy' nuns do the same, spurning the traditional habit which is noticed instantly, and preferring to disguise themselves as social workers from the welfare department; or we 'restructure', and think we are bringing in the Kingdom. God, I think I'm going to be sick.

Synod strikes me, every time I go, as the most vivid contrast to our canteen at work that I am likely ever to encounter. It is not merely that the saints are all in one and the sinners all in the other. I shouldn't like to bet too much on that. It is simply that they seem to belong to different existences, to different worlds. One world is coarse and dirty and ribald and *real*, while the other is woolly, clean, slightly pompous, and *manifestly irrelevant*.

*Thursday 8 May*

I was disappointed that a split-shift prevented me attending any of the Ascension Day services, for I delight in the triumph and glory of this festival. Never mind the poetic spacial metaphors! He came down at Christmas, and he returned whence he came at Ascensiontide, carrying our human nature and human experience into the heart of the Godhead. 'A cloud received him out of their sight' – but it did not conceal us from his sight:

Him though highest heaven receives,
Still he loves the earth he leaves;
Though returning to his throne,
Still he calls mankind his own.

See! He lifts his hands above;
See! He shows the prints of love;
Hark! His gracious lips bestow
Blessings on his church below.

Charles Wesley

Crucified and crowned, 'he ever liveth to make intercession' for us. 'Seeing then that we have a great high priest, that is passed into the heavens, Jesus the Son of God, let us hold fast our profession. For we have not an high priest which cannot be touched with the feeling of our infirmities; but was in all points tempted like as we are, yet without sin. Let us therefore come boldly unto the throne of grace, that we may obtain mercy, and find grace to help in time of need.'

Jesus, the Conqueror, reigns,
In glorious strength arrayed,
His kingdom over all maintains,
And bids the earth be glad.

Extol his kingly power,
Kiss the exalted Son,
Who died; and lives, to die no more,
High on his Father's throne;

Our Advocate with God,
He undertakes our cause,
And spreads through all the earth abroad
The victory of his Cross.

Charles Wesley

*Friday 9 May*

*God is gone up with a merry noise: and the Lord with the sound of the trump.*

*O sing praises, sing praises unto our God: O sing praises, sing praises unto our King.*

Apple blossom; buttercups; pink-edged daisies.

I stopped the bus on the edge of the city this morning when I saw a young hedgehog wandering in circles in the middle of the road. Tony picked it up (with the aid of a handkerchief) and released it on a nearby piece of waste-ground. (I have been known to stop a bus – traffic permitting – and run back up the road to carry a toad to safety!)

*Saturday 10 May*

I noticed one small gorse bush, standing amid others, which was covered in flowers that seemed particularly brilliant – deep, blazing golden-yellow, almost too bright to stare at for more than a second.

I thought immediately of Moses in the desert: 'And the angel of the Lord appeared unto him in a flame of fire out of the midst of a bush: and he looked, and, behold, the bush burned with fire, and the bush was not consumed.'

*Sunday 11 May*

After a special commemoration service this evening, I kissed an old woman who had spent hours preparing the church for the great occasion. It was a spontaneous 'Thank you', and conveyed more than any brief speech. I mention the incident only because immediately there appeared several more who obviously would also have liked to have been kissed. How terrible it must be never to be kissed, or only rarely.

*Monday 12 May*

This month's book is *The Mill on the Floss* by George Eliot. I can't resist one quotation from Mrs Poyser:

'But I suppose you must *be* a Methodist to know what a Methodist 'ull do. It's ill guessing what the bats are flying after.'

*Tuesday 13 May*

I cannot pretend to approve of women in the ministry, and I believe recent moves in that direction are another illustration of panic reaction and a desperate desire to appear 'with-it'. I recognize and deplore the fact that down the centuries women have been exploited and treated as chattels, and I rejoice that at last these wicked injustices seem to be ending. The notion of one sex being superior to another is nonsense by any reckoning, and utterly unchristian. But I am not convinced that the sexes are interchangeable – that there are no distinctive functions which (circumstances being normal) belong to one sex rather than another. And as the woman is the indisputable child-bearer, so I believe that the man is the head of the family. Of course marriage is a partnership of co-equals! Who denies it? But a family unit must have a head. Probably ninety-nine times out of a hundred a mutual decision on family policy can be reached, but on that one other occasion someone will need to make the final decision – and I believe it is the man's responsibility so to do. He is the head of the house. I sympathize deeply with women who want to pursue a career in addition to fulfilling the natural role of wife and mother – and thereby are faced with almost

insurmountable handicaps and disadvantages. I am glad to see women engaged in all kinds of work and being given – within the limitations imposed by nature – equality of opportunity. May these trends continue and accelerate, supported by legislation where practicable. 

Yet the sexes are different – physically and emotionally; and that very difference is a source of mutual enrichment. When the difference becomes blurred or obliterated, both sexes are the poorer. It is not a question of superiority and inferiority; it is a question of different, complementary functions. It is this note which needs to be stressed amid the euphoria of women's liberation, and the church should be prepared to bear witness to it. The church is not a business; the church is much more like a family. And I believe a man should be head of the family (not acting as a bully or a dictator, but presiding in love). Although I have tried to remain objective, I have seldom been impressed observing the results of any other arrangement.

*Wednesday 14 May*

*O deliver not the soul of thy turtle-dove unto the multitude of the enemies: and forget not the congregation of the poor for ever.*

I greatly enjoyed a National Theatre production of Bernard Shaw's *Heartbreak House*, and in the darkness scribbled some (approximate) quotations which appealed to me:

'People don't have their virtues and vices in sets – they have them anyhow, all mixed.'

'The happiness of yielding and dreaming instead of persisting and doing . . .'

'Your marriage was a safety match.'

'I don't like to be answered; it confuses me; it discourages me!'

*Thursday 15 May*

I saw my first horse-chestnut tree in full flower this year – easily the event of the day.

*Friday 16 May*

May is a wonderful month! The lilac is beginning to open, and a wren has taken over as the loudest early-morning songster. Today I noted with a thrill of pleasure that the house-martins are back!

I worked a spreadover, and managed to see a National Theatre lunchtime production of Bernard Shaw's short and seldom-seen comedy about marriage, *Overruled*:

'It doesn't matter about your conduct if your principles are alright!'

'To my English mind, passion is not passion without guilt.'

'I may be doing wrong, but I'm doing it in a proper and customary manner.'

'A man's heart is like a sponge – it sops up dirty water as well as clean.'

I faced the second half of my split-shift happily after that!

*Saturday 17 May*

A tendency is developing among Christians to dispense with the funeral service in church and to proceed, instead, straight to the cemetery or crematorium (with instructions to the minister to be brief and to include no hymns in the service). I view this development with disapproval. No sensitive person wishes to prolong or exacerbate the grief of the bereaved, and funeral rites – like all good worship – should combine dignity with warmth, reverence with simplicity. But death is not to be swept under the carpet. It might seem kind to reduce the ritual to a minimum, omit all music, and conduct such obsequies that remain in as informal a fashion possible – but however laudable the motives, such attitudes are mistaken. Death must be faced with that Christian hope and fortitude which are to be found and assimilated through the ministrations of holy church. A short, gentle ceremony is well-intentioned, but the comparatively painless treatment does not go deep enough. The wound eventually heals over, but the infection is still virulent. A full Christian funeral service in church might provoke more tears but the treatment will be real, the healing deep. The tears will be those of cleansing rather than bitterness. I may not be a good Nonconformist for saying so (although by now nothing should surprise you), but the two most impressive, memorable, and spiritually satisfying funerals I ever attended were both solemn requiem masses. The services were long, and the message of the gospel had time to penetrate, and to be felt as well as heard; holy water and incense focused attention upon the coffin at certain times – not away from it; a sermon was preached and holy communion received; the Russian 'Contakion of the Departed' was sung. I have no desire deliberately to be contentious. I want simply to offer testimony that I found these services profoundly meaningful, and moving to a degree; I felt that the church – to use the common term – had 'delivered the goods', and all had received a powerful, healing ministry. 

*Sunday 18 May*
Whitsunday. The collect:

'God, who as at this time didst teach the hearts of thy faithful people, by the sending to them of the light of thy Holy Spirit; Grant us by the same Spirit to have a right judgement in all things, and evermore to rejoice in his holy comfort; through the merits of Christ Jesus our Saviour, who liveth and reigneth with thee, in the unity of the same Spirit, one God, world without end. Amen.'

I heard and then saw a cuckoo this afternoon while watching a football match. Tony was playing in a busmen's match for Norwich against Peterborough depot. Although he scored a beautiful header, we lost 3–2 in extra time.

*Monday 19 May*
Whenever I read church history I always wonder what sides I would have taken in the great disputes. Would I have been a Primitive Methodist or a Wesleyan Methodist? Would I have joined the Methodists or remained an Anglican? Would I have subscribed to the Act of Uniformity or become an Independent? Would I have been a Protestant or remained a Papist? History enables us to see that truth has many faces; the insights of all godly men are our heritage.

*O magnify the Lord our God, and worship him upon his holy hill: for the Lord our God is holy.*

*Tuesday 20 May*
This was what a May day ought to be like! It was far too glorious to spend sitting in a hot cab – but that's life. While crossing the bridge on the way to work at 6 a.m. I saw my first sand-martin of the year. (It was the same date as that on which I saw the first one in 1954.) Later during the morning I saw the first swifts – and suddenly they seemed to be everywhere.

*I will sing unto the Lord as long as I live: I will praise my God while I have my being.*

*Wednesday 21 May*
I was negotiating a ninety-degree left-hand bend in a narrow street

 this morning when a woman tried to overtake on my nearside. As a result she was trapped between the pavement and the bus, and it cost her a dent in her headlamp and the removal of a strip of beading. Although the bus was not marked I was not very pleased. I think women, by and large, don't make very good drivers. They tend to be short on road-sense, and don't read a situation early enough.

Tony and I wrote our accident reports and were about to hand them in. Tony said, 'You'd better read what I've put.' I said, 'No, I won't bother' – but he was so insistent that I became suspicious and read his account. It was as well I did so:

'My driver had positioned the bus to the right of the road, but with very little room on the inside. This woman brought her car through on the inside of us. She stuck her fingers up and my driver was so angry that he deliberately swung into her offside. I think, myself, that it was the SIX pints of lager he had consumed only ten minutes before which made him aggressive. On leaving his cab he repeatedly tried to punch this lady on the nose, and failing to do so, laid one on the young baby sitting in his pram outside a shop. To my mind he should get six months.'

I cuffed his ear, but he had cheered me up. However, I made him write out another report!

*Nevertheless, he helped them for his Name's sake: that he might make his power to be known.*

I attended a production of *The Yeomen of the Guard* – my favourite G. & S.

*Thursday 22 May*

The first red peonies opened today, and I have been out to enjoy the suggestive, heady, satisfying scent.

On my less-inspired days, my idea of heaven is of an eternal, multiple orgasm in a realm heavy with the scent of red peonies, with a choir singing Anglican chants in the background!

*Friday 23 May*

The social and political forces and the religious controversies which produced the Free Churches in the seventeenth and eighteenth centuries have passed into history. They have taken with them most of the reasons for our continuance as separate denominations. Our witness has been borne, the life of both church and nation has been influenced and leavened, our work is largely done. This conviction lies behind my growing awareness that Free Church worship will never recapture a wide appeal. Our approach to worship is in black and white (literally!), and is based upon battles that have been fought and won. Worship which is more 'catholic', however, will survive all the assaults of this curious age. It is more colourful and – regulated by the Christian year – flows from a source infinitely more vital and enduring. 'Catholic' worship seems linked to the round of the seasons and the rhythm of the cosmos. 

Because our services are devoid of colour, movement, symbol, light, and drama, they will increasingly fail to convey God to man, and they will fail to provoke man to his highest activity: worship. It is a colourful age: television is in colour, men's fashions are no longer dull – the very creation itself is a blaze of colour. So copes and frontals and different-coloured stoles have a valid place in worship. Movement is important: children now learn to dance at school, teenagers dance in the café without inhibition. But our services are static. Processions are fun; moving to a lectern alters the visual focus; genuflecting, bowing, and making the sign of the cross involve our bodies in a physical act of worship.

Symbols are everywhere: British Rail, National Bus, road signs, trade-marks. Creeds, crucifixes, censing, pictures, reservation of the Blessed Sacrament, commemoration of the saints and of the Virgin Mary – these are Christian symbols held dear by many, and pregnant with meaning. But perhaps we are too spiritual to need such aids to devotion? Darkness and light are potent symbols. Candles contribute naturally to an atmosphere of worship, while the Holy Ceremonies of Easter Eve are a 'must' next year for anyone who has never experienced the impact of darkness and light in worship.

The supreme Christian drama is the eucharist – which, to our shame, has not that centrality in Free Church worship which is its due. But there are also lesser dramas. Recently I was invited to share in a service during which an old woman scattered flower-petals before the blessed sacrament as it was carried in procession. I have the strongest conviction that many whom these words will have infuriated most wildly would have been as profoundly moved as I.

The Anglican rejection of the Anglican–Methodist conversations reflected no credit on that great communion, and the judgment of history will be a harsh one. That does not alter the fact that in all the Free Churches we are now in great peril. We're not sure where we are – and our road leads nowhere.

*Saturday 24 May*

The religious awakening experienced by John and Charles Wesley at Whitsuntide, 1738, is commemorated by (some) Methodists on this day; it is the nearest thing to a patronal festival to be found in the Free Churches.

I hold them in high honour. They possessed that great spiritual stature which dwarfs denominational barriers. They belong to the whole church.

Where shall my wondering soul begin?
  How shall I all to heaven aspire?
A slave redeemed from death and sin,
  A brand plucked from eternal fire,
How shall I equal triumphs raise,
Or sing my great Deliverer's praise?

O how shall I the goodness tell,
  Father, which Thou to me hast showed?
That I, a child of wrath and hell,
  I should be called a child of God,
Should know, should feel my sins forgiven,
Blest with this antepast of heaven!

Charles Wesley

I spent the day with John and his friend Kevin – my ornithological experts – beside one of the Norfolk Broads. It was cool, blustery, and showery, but I recorded forty-four different species. Our four nest-boxes were occupied, two by great tits, one by blue tits, and the other – most exciting of all – by a pair of nuthatches! Indeed, we spent the greater part of the day watching these handsome birds flying to and from the nest, feeding their young. The other bird which pleased us most was a common sandpiper, a dainty and attractive creature which we watched at close range and saw several times. Although we were not searching for nests, I found a chaffinch's nest with young, and on the ground we discovered a willow-warbler's nest – a beautiful domed construction with a hole in the side through which we could see the young.

It was a rewarding and invigorating day. The chiffchaff sang, and a sedge-warbler scolded incessantly from his favourite alder among the reeds. Fifteen herons stood on posts and trees beside the broad, and one astonished us by flying down and settling momentarily on the water – something we had never before seen. We watched great-crested grebes only a few yards away, and were delighted whenever one of them dived and surfaced with a fish. Their chicks, also, were in the water. I am the humble pupil of my young mentors – therefor I felt pleased with myself when I was the first to spot the blackcap and the long-tailed tits! A female shoveler, escorted by a large brood of chicks, sailed past proudly just as we had packed the camera! A *wonderful* day; it made me human again.

Full list: house-sparrow, wren, chaffinch, greenfinch, goldfinch, sedge-warbler, tree creeper, robin, cormorant, heron, common tern, house-martin, swift, swallow, moorhen, song-thrush, great crested grebe, mute swan, mallard, common sandpiper, black-headed gull, blue tit, starling, reed-bunting, nuthatch, chiffchaff, hedge-sparrow, bullfinch, willow-warbler, goldcrest, great tit, coal-tit, blackbird, kestrel, blackcap, long-tailed tit, pintail, pied wagtail, pheasant, jackdaw, shoveler, wood-pigeon; also, grey lag goose, barnacle goose (semi-domesticated).

*Sunday 25 May*

Trinty Sunday. The collect:

'Almighty and everlasting God, who hast given unto us thy servants grace by the confession of a true faith to acknowledge the glory of the eternal Trinity, and in the power of the Divine Majesty to worship the Unity; We beseech thee, that thou wouldest keep us stedfast in this faith, and evermore defend us from all adversities, who livest and reignest, one God, world without end. Amen.'

In one part of my sermon this morning I drew on Douglas Thompson's article in the 1967 report of the Methodist Missionary Society:

The doctrine of divinely-controlled change, of the God who is always at work and who is making all things new, stems from the Bible revelation of the nature of God. In the nineteenth century men gloried in the doctrine because it seemed to prophesy pleasant things. Now we see that not everything is going our way, do we drop the doctrine and pick our hymns with care, or do we grip the doctrine more firmly and go on saying 'He reigns till he shall have put everything under his feet'? This is the point at which courage is salvation. Wives and sweethearts have lost their men in this woeful century by gas-gangrene and the slow death of prison starvation BUT 'Ancient of days we dwell in Thee'. 

God has not forsaken us! He is ever at work, changing, renewing, and in control.

In the writings of Mao Tse-tung is a saying which likens the guerilla soldier to a fish swimming in the sea of the people. It is impossible to defeat him because if you scoop him out you must scoop out many people with him whom you cannot afford to alienate. If you angle for him individually you need more anglers than fish, and where do you get them? Having caught a fish, how do you know he is the one you want? Bomb the waters and the shock-wave carries him away from the bomb-blast.

So is the believer in the Almighty God among those masses of people who hold that life has no meaning in our changing world. The modern church, distributed in tiny pockets among the nations, is indeed like small shoals of fighter-fish swimming among the aimless fish of the world. It cannot be conquered for the very reasons Mao Tse-tung suggests. It can be harassed, it can be dispersed, it can be held back from securing its objectives, but it cannot be conquered.

Yet that invincibility depends upon the retention of its basic belief just as the communist movement depends upon the same thing. Communism fears most of all what it calls 'revisionism' – by which it means a dilution of basic belief by the encroachment of bourgeois ease and permissiveness: 'it doesn't matter if . . .' This removes the will to struggle. This alone is fatal to the movement.

There is a Christian revisionism, and it is not the departure from the conservative-evangelical, fundamentalist-cum-literalist attitude to the Bible, as is frequently hinted. The Christian revisionism is a departure from the utter conviction that God is the lord of heaven and earth, who directs a plan for humanity and for the whole creation. The church, however scattered and changed, is invincible so long as it contains men who stand in awe of God, the eternal trinity.

As I crossed the bridge from my house to the cathedral this afternoon I saw a kingfisher. Evensong included one of my favourite anthems: John Stainer's 'I saw the Lord'. (I checked, several weeks ago, to make sure it would be sung today!) It is a strong, eight-part

work based upon Isaiah's vision in the temple. In effective contrast to the vigorous opening, the second part begins with the quiet invocation: 

O Trinity! O Unity!
Be present as we worship Thee,
And with the songs that angels sing
Unite the hymns of praise we bring.

After the service a scholarly old priest spoke to me feelingly of what Trinity Sunday meant to him. These were his words, as I remember them:

'Trinity Sunday is the crown of the Christian year. The revelation of God which was made in Christ built upon the Old Testament revelation of the holiness and the unity of the living God. Our Lord revealed that in the one, holy, living, and true God there exists the most astonishing richness of being and personality.

Beginning with the preparation of Advent – the gathering-up of law-giver, prophet, and wise-man – the Christian year celebrates the incarnate life and word, the passion and resurrection, and the great days of the presence of the risen Lord with the eleven. It pauses to remember the coming of the Holy Spirit to make the church the body of the living Christ – and one starts to ask, "Who-ever is this God we've seen in Christ?" Trinity Sunday supplies the answer. God is true, utter, whole, infinite, unity; unity who is also diversity. And we spend the rest of the year worshipping and serving this living God in his holiness and threefold unity.

It is this diversity in unity which is the key to him who is utter being, the key to the whole creation, and the key to man's life within the creation. God and his works possess and display a most strange wholeness. The creation reflects the wholeness as well as the holiness of God, and the gospel – the living word of the living God – is whole-making. The mission of the Holy Spirit and the purpose of the church is to make men whole. God made man whole, but man "went to pieces" – became disjointed, disorientated, alienated. Modern man is feeling for that wholeness which is his true nature. Trinity Sunday – the octave-day of Whitsun, concluding Pentecost week – shows where it is to be found: in relationship – at one – with the God whose creation displays a glorious galaxy of diversity in its wholeness, and who himself is trinity in unity. That is the gospel. That is the Catholic faith. And that is why Trinity Sunday is the crown of the Christian year.'

*Monday 26 May*

'There is always, somewhere, an injured creature who prevents me being happy' – From Anouilh's *La Sauvage*.

*Tuesday 27 May*

The irony of the following incident was not lost on me, and I smiled: by slowing down for a woman I recognized who was running for the bus, I prevented a prostitute being late for work this evening.

*Wednesday 28 May*

The rhododendrons in one of the city parks present a striking picture, while gardens and hedgerows are decked with may-blossom, laburnum, and lilac. The daisies are so thick in the churchyard they resemble a fall of snow. This month has seen a tremendous change in the appearance of the garden: suddenly, everything has grown tall. Today I saw an orange-tip butterfly.

*Thursday 29 May*

The feast of Corpus Christi. I went to mass before starting my shift. Even as I received the most holy sacrament I gave thanks for the precious food by which our souls are nourished with the risen life of Christ.

Angels and men might strive in vain,
They could not add the smallest grain
  T'augment Thy death's atoning power;
The sacrifice is all complete
The death Thou never canst repeat,
  Once offered up to die no more.

Yet may we celebrate below,
And daily thus Thine offering show
  Exposed before Thy Father's eyes;
In this tremendous mystery
Present Thee bleeding on a tree,
  Our everlasting Sacrifice.

Charles Wesley

*Friday 30 May*

*He healeth those that are broken in heart: and giveth medicine to heal their sickness.*

*He telleth the number of the stars: and calleth them all by their names.*

*Great is our Lord, and great is his power: yea, and his wisdom is infinite.*

*The Lord setteth up the meek: and bringeth the ungodly down to the ground.*

*Saturday 31 May*

Unhappily, buses are involved in fatal accidents occasionally, and a particularly horrible fatality occurred during the rush-hour last evening, when a woman was run over. It was the main topic of (curiously subdued) conversation in the garage today, when sympathy for the victim and her relatives was combined with sympathy for the driver and conductor. Such accidents seem briefly to enhance our sense of brotherhood; for this is the thing you never think about, yet always dread.

Tonight Tony and I did a late trip to Yarmouth. We just had time to eat some chips on the jetty before leaving on the return run at 10.30. I was reminded of my last trip down here in the autumn. The sea was not rough this evening, but in the darkness its spell was sure: Tony said, 'I like being by the sea at night, like this.'

*Sunday 1 June*

Between leaving Yarmouth Bus Station at 10.30 last night and climbing the steps of the pulpit at 10.30 this morning, I had driven a bus to Norwich, walked home, eaten supper and gone to bed, breakfasted, and written an article. This evening I was glad to accept an invitation to share in a service of evensong, procession, and benediction, as part of the Corpus Christi celebrations in a neighbouring parish where one of the few bus drivers with church connections is churchwarden.

*Monday 2 June*

*I will sing of the Lord, because he hath dealt so lovingly with me: yea, I will praise the Name of the Lord most Highest.*

I must be a miserable hypocrite. The summer is coming, and the holidaymakers are upon us, and I decided at evensong that I liked the winter best. What am I running on about? Tourists – and the theological difference between Sunday and midweek worship. On Sundays and special occasions, visitors are not allowed to wander about that part of the cathedral which is in use during divine service. A noticeably more lenient view is taken during the week – and highly distracting are the results. Not for the first time, a camera was in action beside me tonight. If I had dashed it to the ground would I have cleansed the temple? I appreciate and sympathize with the intentions of those who are glad to have visitors strolling around. Indeed, those intentions are much after my own heart! The theory is that as the sightseers stumble upon the worship they may pause to listen, and something in the prayers and the music may arrest them. I repeat: I understand this hope (and feel guilty for not entering into it fully); yet I reject it.

Despite their antiquity and their treasures, cathedrals are not museums; they are centres of living worship. And that worship is of the same essential, holy, quality whether it is offered on Sunday morning or Monday evening. Let us invite people to join the congregation; let us permit them, encourage them, plead with them! But if that is not their desire, they ought not to be allowed to wander about and become a distraction for those who wish to worship. They are not helped by our rating reverence so low.

I, too, long for people to catch a glimpse of God. That is why, at the present moment, I live 'in the world' in the manner I have adopted. But it is no game. After eight hours at the wheel I need – as a matter of urgency – the quiet and the refreshment of worship to still my spirit and recharge my depleted resources. Much of that help I find in the daily services of the cathedral. This is the ministry it exists to offer: worship to God, and strong consolation to the man seeking God. That ministry is muted (rightly or wrongly) by cameras, footsteps, and whispered conversations. When these are permitted during Sunday services and special concerts, I will try to persuade myself that all is for the best during the week.

Thus disgruntled, and muttering darkly, I went – a little later – to lock the door of our parish church for the night. Before doing so, I had first to clear up a stinking lump of human excrement which had been discharged on to the floor of the church. I do not believe that men and women are just ignorant, and victims of society, and at the mercy of their genes. When every generous allowance has been made I believe, also, that they are wicked.

*Tuesday 3 June*

The old priest who thrilled me on Trinity Sunday had more words of wisdom for me today in the form of a quotation from St Ignatius Loyola: 'No great work can be done, worthy of God, without earth in an uproar and hell's legions roused.'

*Wednesday 4 June*

To say that life is a paradox is to say nothing original or profound. The experience – for which none of us asked – seems an insoluble jumble of conflicts and confusions within which various aspects of 'truth' contradict each other, and vie with one another for our allegiance. What is this fleeting experience we have been given – this gift which soon will be reclaimed? Is life a serious business? Or is it a joke?

Much of life is undeniably sobering; much resembles a second-rate farce. A friend, in cynical mood, recently remarked: 'The universe is one big laugh – and the joke's on us.' At times it can seem a sick joke; then we are not sure whether to laugh or cry.

I am as convinced that there is humour and divine incongruity at the heart of the Godhead as I am convinced there is burning love. Our antics must cause convulsions of laughter in heaven. We are so puny, and so full of self-importance.

Yet to be minuscule and relatively insignificant is not necessarily to be worthless. On the the contrary, I cannot help believing that God has given a potential to every person which makes that person unique and precious beyond compare. He has given a portion of the eternal divine spirit – and it is this which transforms each man and woman into a being of infinite value.

*Thursday 5 June*

Tony had a minor operation on his arm on Monday, so he's off work this week. However much I enjoy a shift with somebody else (and many of the men are excellent company), it isn't the same as working with one's regular mate.

On the bus at the terminus this morning, a woman aged about fifty said to me, 'Are you fast?' (She was referring, one must assume, either to my watch or my driving.) I fixed her a wicked, knowing look and whispered hoarsely: 'Fast? I shall have kissed *you* before we get to the station!' 'My God!' she exclaimed – either in horror or anticipation. But, of course, I'm all talk . . .

When other people do things, it's easy to see how wrong they are; yet if I want to do something similar I can soon find extenuating circumstances.

A beautiful, warm summer's evening. It demanded a drink.

*Friday 6 June*

When he realized I was a Methodist, the conductor I was with today said: 'My mother was a Methodist. I can remember her and my grandmother singing a hymn. It went like this:

'Twas just a hundred years ago,
When on Mow Hill there stood
A little band, with hearts aflame
To preach Redeeming Blood;
Singing, "Glory! Hallelujah!
The Lord is with us still" –
And that little band increaseth,
That grew upon Mow Hill.

I've always wondered where Mow Hill was.'

So I told him. It was surprising suddenly to have that old Primitive Methodist song from a different generation produced in the canteen. We had an interesting discussion on the influence of Primitive Methodism among the working-classes, and I told him about Robert Key who missioned and transformed the Watton, Mattishall, and East Dereham area of mid-Norfolk.

*I will inform thee, and teach thee in the way wherein thou shalt go: and I will guide thee with mine eye.*

*Saturday 7 June*

The hot day brought cruel torment! I drove to Lowestoft; the beach beckoned, but our duty allowed exactly one minute before the start of the return journey! It wasn't worth switching off the engine.

At a concert in the cathedral tonight I preferred the Haydn (Little Organ Mass) to the Britten and Bernstein.

*Sunday 8 June*

Two 'bus' baptisms at the morning service; then I worked a late shift. During conversation, the conductor asserted that one of the important things missing from life today was a sense of companionship: '. . . the kind of companionship we knew in the army during the war. If you had a fag and your mate didn't, you gave him half; if you had some money and he didn't, you shared it with him; if you were going out somewhere but he had to work late, you got his things ready for him.'

I remember a driver saying something similar, referring to the days long before the war when he was a young conductor: 'If I found any money on the bus I always gave half to the driver; it didn't matter if it was only a penny, he'd have a halfpenny of it. That's how we worked in those days.'

Things haven't changed entirely. Recently, Tony received a substantial reward for some lost property he'd handed in – and gave half to me without hesitation. It depends upon the quality of the relationship as well as the spirit of the age.

But there has been a vast change in attitudes since the war. Charlie – who, incidentally, has been a server for fifty years – was adamant about it tonight: 'Passengers used to be much more friendly and good natured than they seem today. We're better off now, but moan and groan a lot more. And there's not that companionship.' I suspect he may be right. It's tragic if we can't have what he calls 'companionship' without conscription or a war.

Charlie told two good stories. One day, a full-bosomed woman was running for the waiting bus. Another regular female passenger – with a voice which could be heard all over the vehicle – surveyed her as she clambered aboard, and remarked: 'Come you on now, Edna. If you run like that you'll get your bleedin' tits twisted round your necklace!'

On a trip from Mattishall in a blizzard, Charlie's bus became stuck in the snow. After a long wait in the stranded vehicle, the call of nature became too strong for three old women, and they went round the back of the bus. 'When the first one stood up, we heard such a blood-curdling shriek we wondered whatever had happened. But we needn't have worried too much: the wind had filled her knickers full of snow.'

*Monday 9 June*

My conductor (on a late shift) was a leading member of the branch committee, so we had long discussions on Union matters; it was just like old times!

On sunny evenings around midsummer the appearance of the city seems altered completely by the sun shining brightly from the ex-

treme west, casting long shadows and highlighting buildings usually in shade. It was a pleasure to be in the streets. 

But the day had been hot. At the edge of the city, on the last run tonight, I pulled the cab window fully open to smell the night. A light breeze blew across the fields, bearing with it an invigorating fragrance. If I am insane, it's rather pleasant.

*Tuesday 10 June*

I had the same conductor as last Friday. His first words were: 'There's another old hymn I remember. They used to sing it at the Seaman's Bethel I went to. It's called "Pull for the Shore". Do you know it?' Happily, my broad and genuine catholicity enabled me to claim that I *was*, in fact, acquainted with that particular number – and I sang a few lines to prove it!

*Wednesday 11 June*

It was a hot and busy day on the bus. I enjoy sunshine, but soon wilt in hot weather, and I couldn't get to the pub quick enough after work.

There was a great fire in our street today which gutted an attractive eighteenth-century house which had been restored only recently. I watched despondently as flames leapt from the windows. I think I prefer Georgian houses to Tudor gables and half-timbered cottages. The grace of proportion and simplicity of design – with Corinthian capitals and pedimented doorways – is appealing and satisfying.

*Thursday 12 June*

Lupins are my favourite flowers (not blue ones), and they are now at their most magnificent.

By the roadside: foxgloves; red clover; white clover; bladder campion; ox-eye daisies.

I really suffer on these boiling hot days.

It is interesting to see how people who have been sunbathing turn different shades, from rich bronze to the dusky brown of ripe wheat.

*Friday 13 June*

Two impressions gained during a shift: the sight of the market flower-stalls laden with pyrethrums and sweet williams . . . the good and wholesome smell of bread being baked.

*But let all those that seek thee be joyful and glad in thee: and let all such as delight in thy salvation say alway, The Lord be praised.*

'Have I ever done you any harm? Have I ever hurt you, cheated you, treated you meanly, or been deliberately unkind in any way?'

'No.'

'Have I tried, sometimes, to show kindness; and tried, occasionally, to be generous?'

'Yes.'

'If – at least – we are agreed on those things, I don't really care what else you think of me: because nothing else matters very much.' – From an imaginary conversation!

*Saturday 14 June*

I had a day in the country to unwind. I returned with a colourful and gorgeously-scented bouquet of lilac, honeysuckle, philadelphus, lupins, double marigolds, red and white campion, yellow flags, and wild parsley.

At a party tonight I watched, almost mesmerized, as two girls in black danced with each other. I know nothing about dancing – I've ruined the odd Gay Gordons now and again, but that's the extent of my experience. This, however, was powerful stuff. The dancers never touched, yet were in perfect balance and affinity. Their movements were urgent and expressive yet graceful and controlled, and they created a communion between themselves which was intense and beautiful and utterly fascinating. The wonder of movement! Others looked cumbersome by comparison; these I could have watched all night.

*Sunday 15 June*

There appears to be a clash of culture in our house. To my son's horror, his mother thought Purcell was the washing-powder she'd used for years.

The canticles at evensong were sung to one of my favourite settings: Purcell in G minor.

I tried to catch Trevor today, and found he could run faster than I. It was another of those sobering and revealing moments!

*Monday 16 June*

*My soul hath a desire and longing to enter into the courts of the Lord: my heart and my flesh rejoice in the living God.*

Richard Baxter's great hymn 'He wants not friends that hath Thy love' was sung at evensong to the tune 'O Jesu mi dulcissime'. I would like this sung at my funeral, together with Isaac Watts' 'Give me the wings of faith to rise', (sung to 'Mylon'); Charles Wesley's 'Come, let us join our friends above', (sung to 'St Matthew'); the Russian Contakion; and lots of other wonderful things, all of which I hope to hear and enjoy. 

*Tuesday 17 June*

A young tree in fresh foliage – with its bark completely peeled off by vandals – had an extraordinarily depressing effect on me.

*Lord, how long wilt thou hide thyself, for ever?*

*Wednesday 18 June*

Only flickers of faith and the most vague longings for God are possible in us. We cannot *know* God in the way that we know the man next door, or last week's football results. If we *could* know God with that earthly brand of certainty, human life would become impossible. We would be able to concentrate on nothing else. Not for an instant would God leave our thoughts. Normal activity would cease.

Thus, within our wonderful little bodies of mud, we are sheltered from the overwhelming, all-devouring impact of God's unshielded glory. We have not been given adequate apparatus with which to bear the brightness of his immediate presence. We need protection from God's unspeakable splendour. In love he hides himself, he veils himself, he withdraws to give us a life of our own, not swamped by his intensity. There is blessing in his remoteness.

Yet the creator Spirit delights in being known, and is revealing himself constantly to those who will receive truth, in precious moments of insight and illumination. There is sweet ecstasy to taste and enjoy when the veil is drawn aside and a glance of divine light stabs through the darkness of our minds, and speaks of God. Large doses would be more than flesh and blood could endure; but these foretastes have an intensity and depth of meaning which liberate the spirit, transfigure life with sacredness and significance – and make us long for more.

*Thursday 19 June*

However pressed for time I am, I can't resist looking quickly at the garden at this time of the year, very early in the morning before I go to work. The roses are my chief attraction, and the hedge of

 Nevada, Chinatown, Albertine, and Scarlachglut looks superb. Fragrant Cloud and Mischief are the best of the hybrid teas at the moment, with Josephine Bruce a mass of deep, dusky-red roses which look as if they have been fashioned from some exquisite velvet.

*O sing unto the Lord a new song: for he hath done marvellous things.*

*Friday 20 June*

This was a hot and busy day, with Tony collecting his highest takings on the buses to date. It was a split shift, and this evening we took the same bus back to the garage that we brought out this morning. The hottest part of a hot day is 2 p.m. until 6 p.m., and this afternoon – with full loads – we both sweltered.

After a pint tonight, I stood on the bridge and enjoyed a pipe, and tried to ease the tension out of my system. It was ten o'clock but still warm. Fish were rising, and a bat flittered to and fro. The sky towards the west was flushed with rose, and for me this was the best time of the day. I strolled into the burial ground of The Old Meeting House. The three-quarter moon had brightened; masses of elder flowers hung in creamy clusters. After the heat, and noise, and activity, all was still.

*Saturday 21 June*

Summer solstice.

I received a postcard from a friend visiting Assisi, who clearly had fallen under the spell of that town: '. . . How cold and pale the religion of the English is in comparison . . .' The postcard featured that paean of praise by St Francis, 'The Canticle of the Creatures':

'Most high omnipotent good Lord, to Thee praise, glory, honour, and every benediction.
To Thee alone Most High do they belong.
And no man is worthy to pronounce Thy Name.
Praise be to Thee my Lord with all Thy creatures.
Especially for Master Brother Sun who illuminates the day for us, And Thee Most High he manifests.
Praise be to Thee my Lord for Sister Moon and for the stars, in Heaven Thou hast formed them, shining, precious, fair.
Praise be to Thee my Lord for Brother Wind, for air and clouds, clear sky and all the weathers through which Thou sustainest all Thy creatures.

Praise be to Thee my Lord for Sister Water; she is useful and humble, precious and pure.
Praise be to Thee my Lord for Brother Fire; through him our night Thou dost enlighten, and he is fair and merry, boisterous and strong.
Praise be to Thee my Lord for our sister Mother Earth, who nourishes and sustains us all, bringing forth divers fruits and many-coloured flowers and herbs.
Praise be to Thee my Lord for those who pardon grant for love of Thee and bear infirmity and tribulation.
Blessed be those who live in peace, for by Thee Most High they shall be crowned.
Praise be to Thee my Lord for our Sister Bodily Death from whom no living man can flee; woe to them who die in mortal sin but blessed they who shall be found in Thy most holy Will;
To them the second death can do no harm.
O bless and praise my Lord all creatures, and thank and serve Him in deep humility.'

*Sunday 22 June*

Boys were catching eels by the bridge at lunchtime. I have a great reverence for eels. That each one should have crossed the Atlantic is almost beyond belief.

I preached this morning, went to evensong this afternoon, and worked a late shift tonight.

By now it will be balefully obvious to everyone that I do not solve industrial crises, that I am not consulted daily on matters of policy, that the pastoral work arising from my presence in industry is comparatively limited, and (you suspected correctly) I don't try very hard to get people to come to church. 'At last! He's broken and confessed,' you cry with glee. 'Now he must come back in, and do the job he was called to do.'

Why this excitement? I would have made the same confession last 2 September, had you asked. (I was mellow enough, in all truth.) Indeed, it was largely to this very end that I began to write. All I claim is that at least I am *there*; getting increasingly muddied, maybe, but *there*.

Although it sounds presumptious, I have tried to give myself to the world. I may not have given much, but I've given what I am.

I try to provide one small point of acceptance and warmth, constantly and unconditionally. I could have been elsewhere, but I chose this: simply to live in a certain way in a certain place. Is there no way in which the meaning of 'ordained ministry' can be stretched to cover this?

My tongue is in my cheek! I believe, of course, that no stretching is needed. I find it much harder to stretch ministry to cover other things which are regarded as an integral part of the traditional ministry. But I've not much energy to argue any more. As I may already have said, ultimately either you see it or you don't.

*Monday 23 June*

This month's book: Plato's *The Symposium.*

*Tuesday 24 June*

Midsummer day.

I walked through the old cemetery which gradually is being 'tidied'. I know many of the trees 'personally'. I resent the tidying. Graves covered with undergrowth, which made death seem natural and undramatic, have been laid bare – and their starkness is disturbing. Those who have torn away the ivy and tall grass and shrubs have made death slightly more frightening to me.

The family to whom one large grave belongs have refused permission for it to be cleared. 'Just look at it,' said the keeper. 'Doesn't it look terrible?' But I thought it looked terrific and murmured secretly, 'Three cheers for them!' And the birds agreed. One pathway, not yet cleared, looked especially beautiful in the morning sunshine, and I was deeply stirred. Here the song-thrush had his anvil.

A wonderful evensong tonight, a veritable feast of fat things. Stanford in C.

*Blessed are they that keep his testimonies: and seek him with their whole heart.*

*Wednesday 25 June*

We had a coach instead of a double-decker this afternoon. At one point our only passengers were two good-natured women in their fifties who hailed from somewhere up north. One said to the other, 'I hope you'll be all right with these two when I get off the bus.' Then, as she alighted, she called back to her friend: 'Watch what you're up to, Agnes. If you get too much, send me a bit.' This was all totally lost on me, of course, but after my conductor had explained (!!) I couldn't help wondering if there was another minister in the country who today had been the subject of similar remarks.

*Thursday 26 June*

I do not swear involuntarily very often. I don't much like to hear it. Usually it displays a poverty of vocabulary and an undisciplined spirit. But a problem of communication is involved. I was discussing the subject with an education officer over a drink recently, and he was of the same opinion. Each swear-word, and each inflection with which it is uttered, conveys a distinct and precise shade of meaning, harder to capture in conventional Queen's English than might be imagined. For example, you can say 'Go away' with all the emphasis at your command, but I doubt if you will communicate the various nuances of meaning which are possible if you say – well, you know . . .

*Friday 27 June*

Though I am rarely late, etc., I used to worry a little if I did anything wrong at work, fearing it would impair my 'witness'. I needn't have bothered. I have found that an occasional mistake causes unbounded delight, and convinces others that you're human after all. Witness is only impaired seriously by failures in love: by impatience, harsh criticism, and having no time to listen. Having been a bus driver for seven years now puts me squarely among the regulars – the turn-over of staff is high. The fact that I am ex-chairman of the branch compensates for any remaining deficiencies in my length of service, and gives me a degree of acceptance which once would have been beyond my wildest dreams. It is a cultural/sociological breakthrough I would not surrender lightly.

*Saturday 28 June*

A priest is human. A priest has feelings. A priest knows temptation. Sermon prepation. Words, words, words. Keep churning them out. I feel like poor Jack Point, the merryman in *The Yeomen of the Guard*:

Though your head it may rack with a bilious attack,
　And your senses with toothache you're losing,
Don't be mopy and flat – they don't fine you for that,
　If you're properly quaint and amusing!

Though your wife ran away with a soldier that day,
And took with her your trifle of money;
Bless your heart, they don't mind – they're exceedingly kind –
They don't blame you – as long as you're funny!

*Sunday 29 June*

The Prodigal Son:

Religion, high principles, and a strong sense of duty such as the loyal elder brother displayed can be noble virtues; but if pride and hardness of heart creep in, they can become terrible things. They can put our souls in jeopardy. Be on guard.

The carelessness, self-centredness, and thoughtlessness showed by the young man when first he left home are signposts on the road to misery: yet some who are plainly on that road are capable of displaying flashes of tenderness, compassion, sensitivity, and humility of which the righteous never dream. They may conceivably be nearer the heart of the Father than many of us who stand and recite creeds.

In Glasgow there are hundreds of down-and-outs. In the city centre is the well-known church of St George's, Tron, which stands in Buchanan Street. One morning I wanted to look round that church. I entered the vestibule, but could not get into the church itself. The inner doors seemed locked, though looking through a window in one of them I could see one of those ragged down-and-outs seated inside. I searched for a door which was unlocked, but I couldn't find one. How on earth had *he* got in? I never found out. I glared through the window at the scruffy figure inside, and I was angry.

*Monday 30 June*

I saw a pair of kestrels hovering above the aerodrome – an excellent start to a Monday morning.

I seldom adopt a judgmental attitude towards any of my workmates, although occasionally I check myself only just in time. I nearly broke my rule today when I witnessed a piece of gross rudeness to a person who clearly had intended no offence. I felt ashamed of my silence; yet it was deliberate. It is easy to rebuke – and destroy a relationship, all to no advantage. Usually, it is better to keep silent and retain that deeper link of trust which makes a ministry of acceptance viable and full of potential. It is compromise of the kind I detest most, because it seems to contaminate by acquiescence. But I have learned this lesson the hard way. It is always more difficult to accept the unlovely: yet it may be to them, beneath their rough ways, that your friendship means most.

Psalm 148 – sung tonight at evensong – is very precious to me:

*O praise the Lord of heaven: praise him in the height.*
*Praise him, all ye angels of his: praise him, all his host.*
*Praise him, sun and moon: praise him, all ye stars and light.*
*Praise him, all ye heavens: and ye waters that are above the heavens.*
*Let them praise the Name of the Lord: for he spake the word, and they were made; he commanded, and they were created.*
*He hath made them fast for ever and ever: he hath given them a law which shall not be broken.*
*Praise the Lord upon earth: ye dragons, and all deeps;*
*Fire and hail, snow and vapours: wind and storm, fulfilling his word;*
*Mountains and all hills: fruitful trees and all cedars;*
*Beasts and all cattle: worms and feathered fowls;*
*Kings of the earth and all people: princes and all judges of the world;*
*Young men and maidens, old men and children, praise the Name of the Lord: for his Name only is excellent, and his praise above heaven and earth.*
*He shall exalt the horn of his people; all his saints shall praise him: even the children of Israel, even the people that serveth him.*

*Tuesday 1 July*

I saw a distant cousin the other day, and marvelled at how closely his features resembled those of his grandmother. It must be twenty-five years since she died, yet to see her grandson is instantly to be reminded of her. I couldn't help thinking that in one sense we are not, each one of us, new creations: we are extended creations. So much of our mental/physical/emotional make-up comes directly from our parents, who received theirs from their parents, and so on ad infinitum. The further back we go the more we discover that we are related to each other. We share a common humanity. The sins and the triumphs of people long ago pass into the nature of the race and affect the attitudes and the appearances of generations to come; our own actions and our own decisions do likewise. Truly we are members one of another; we belong to each other in far more than a moral or theological sense – we belong to each other physically. One might almost be tempted to wonder if there is, in fact, any such thing as an individual person – or only humanity en masse: one continuing, ever-renewing organism called man.

But there is, of course, another side to the picture. I saw a boy who had been involved in an accident, and had had his leg amputated. Never again would he be able to play football. That which he had lost would never be restored to him. For he is unique; what has been taken has been taken for ever. No matter, to him, how many million pairs of legs in perfect working order exist elsewhere among the human race: his have been impaired, and nothing can alter the fact, or put the matter right. However much truth there is in the view that humanity is one, it is not the whole truth. The mass is flecked with individual centres of consciousness, distinct awarenesses, separate existences – each one unique in its combinations of characteristic, and each (we would want to say) of unique 'worth'.

Another thing interests me: I like to look at the face of a young person and imagine the way in which the features will develop into the maturity of middle and old age. The reverse process is even more striking. To look at an old person, and to see the marks of the years vanish away – revealing the eager, innocent features of youth – is to increase in true sympathy. To become aware that an aged person, though weighted by physical limitations, still thinks and feels in much the same way as those who, as yet, retain their full faculties, is to grow in warmth and tenderness. To see old women as little girls, and youths as old men, is to permit the imagination to stimulate within us a greater sensitivity and affection.

On a wall in our house is an old photograph of one of the most handsome women I have ever seen. It is a portrait of my wife's grandmother, taken when she was a young women. She was almost one hundred years old when she died a few years ago – and when the portrait hung in her cottage, I always found it moving to compare the photograph with the little wrinkled old woman sitting by the fire. The body changes – yet retains an essence which is constant.

The manner in which flesh is continually renewed is yet another mystery. A year before my birth there was no sign of me, yet the chemical elements which at various times have constituted my body were presumably in existence somewhere. From my mother I received a body, composed of chemicals she had obtained from food and air and water; I have nourished that body in the same way, and it has developed and matured. I read that the body renews itself completely every seven years. The shape is recognizable, but ever changing. It grows strong, then becomes weak. And it consists, all the while, of chemicals, of dust, of elements which we absorb from the creation around us. 'Dust thou art, and unto dust shalt thou return.' When we die, the elements constituting our physical body at that particular moment return again quickly to the earth, to assume new shapes and forms. It is all very awesome, and wonderful, and mysterious.

I mention all these things for one reason. I have no stunning summary. I want simply to exclaim, once more, how strange is this gift of life that we have received, and how matter-of-fact modern man has become in the face of the mystery! Our bodies return to the dust; but what of the people who expressed themselves through those forms – who knew temptation and experienced love? What of the 'spirit'? Our faith is in one who assumed human fashion and was unashamed to express himself in a human body. Upon him is based the Christian hope that our destiny is with God.

*Wednesday 2 July*

The sad fields awaiting development have displayed one last glorious flash of defiance. Untouched this year by chemical sprays, they are a solid and spectacular blaze of blood-red poppies, such as now is rarely seen.

A conductor passing through a period of intense worry mentioned some of his difficulties, and I admired the courage with which he was attempting to deal with them. Suddenly he said: 'Joking apart – give us a prayer.' That is an illustration of the meaning of 'presence'.

Evensong and procession for the Visitation of the Blessed Virgin Mary:

*The Lord looked down from heaven upon the children of men: to see if there were any that would understand, and seek after God.*

Great excitement at tea time! Our large yellow underwing moth emerged from its chrysalis and climbed up the television set to a vase of sweet williams and cornflowers. There it hung, while life flowed slowly into its wings. It is possible only to experience reverence before such a wonder.

I am going into the church now, to keep my promise and 'give him a prayer'.

*Thursday 3 July*

I am reading *Anna of the Five Towns* by Arnold Bennett.

*Friday 4 July*

Tony is on holiday in Spain. Today I received a postcard addressed to 'The Rt. Rev.' He knows flattery never fails, and that it will be my turn to get the teas in when he returns.

Today's conductor – an apostate Salvationist bandsman of nineteen – had a dry sense of humour which I enjoyed. When I informed him that my suit was bought in Sauchiehall Street in 1963, he replied, thoughtfully: 'Ah yes, '63 – a very good year for suits.'

*But thy loving-kindness and mercy shall follow me all the days of my life: and I will dwell in the house of the Lord for ever.*

*Saturday 5 July*

A day in the country. I spent the morning scything a large area of garden which had been left fallow, and where an amazing variety of wild flowers and grasses had grown vigorously. As my companion remarked, reviewing my labours: 'Our Lord's command was taken too literally in this garden.' Then, as an afterthought: 'Except by those raspberries . . .'

Once I have settled into a steady rhythm, I enjoy scything and find it satisfying; but to think the harvest once was gathered this way . . . The bullfinches watched with anguish as their favourite weed-seeds disappeared, and vowed that the fruit-tree buds in this garden would receive particular attention next spring in an act of calculated retribution. The sun grew hot, and I stripped to the waist and ordered refreshment. As the scythe swished through the grass I savoured all kinds of marvellous thoughts, as in a dream: people, and love, and gardens, and Our Lady. I noticed that different scents appeared as the scythe cut through different plants. Then, as my back began to ache, the job was done: everything was cleared except a large patch of purple loosestrife I could not bring myself to cut and had carefully avoided! Down to the village pub, post haste . . .!

Impressions of the day:

Field scabious, dog rose, yellow water-lily, and fragrant meadowsweet. Ivy-leaved toadflax on the wall; alstroemeria and lilium regale in the garden.

A pair of swans with their cygnets; a swallows' nest with young in the village bus shelter; a skylark soaring into the sky, singing as though its very existence depended upon the volume and continuity of its song. 

Country conversation:

Earnest Nonconformist schoolteacher in the early '30s on the evils of masturbation: 'Who but a fool would sacrifice eternity for the sake of titillating a nerve?'

'When I worked in the hospital I had to wash the old men. One was fast becoming senile, but he combined senility with unusual discernment! One morning he said to me: "You're new here, aren't you?" "No," I replied, "I washed you yesterday." "No, you didn't," he said. "It was that great lout with a wart on the back of his neck." '

'Never mind about getting your hands dirty – don't you realize that one of the last actions performed by our Lord during his Resurrection appearances was to gut fish?'

'One for the rook, One for the crow, One to die, And one to grow.' – Old rhyme.

*Sunday 6 July*

Today was the tenth anniversary of my ordination to the Methodist ministry.

Throughout the seven years of my 'worker-priest' ministry I have been based – in an ecumenical gesture – at an Anglican church, and the double failure of the Anglican-Methodist Unity Conversations (1969 and 1972) was a bitter blow. I had seen this union as vital to the mission of the church in England, and had worked hard for its acceptance. At a personal level, the scheme would have enabled me to share equally in the ministry of the church to which I was attached; even more significant, I knew that – for me – a more solid liturgical fare and a greater sacramental emphasis were becoming matters of urgency. From my earliest days as a Christian, I had mourned over the ugly plainness of the Free Church ethos which made God as remote as excessive ritual.

How was the impasse to be resolved? In November 1972 the *Methodist Recorder* gave prominence to an article in which I urged the ministers of Methodism to break the Anglican-Methodist deadlock, and for the sake of the gospel make a supreme, sacrificial act of commitment, and graciously submit to re-ordination. In 1973 I made application to the President of the Conference for permission

'to seek episcopal ordination as an extension but in no way a denial of my present ministry'. Failing to receive a straight answer either way, I proceeded with a clear conscience, but failed twice in attempts to secure Anglican orders. If I resigned from Methodism I might become acceptable to the Church of England – but that would be a step sideways, not forward. I do not intend to resign. I cannot and will not deny my Methodist heritage; but I want to be an Anglican priest – and, please God, before I die, a priest once more in communion with the see of Rome.

I have no wish to abjure my Methodism; I want to carry it forward into a new and larger context. I would find it hard, however, to return to the traditional routine of the Methodist ministry. My longing for a more varied diet of worship has become undeniable. I am too much of a historian, too much of an Englishman, and too much of a catholic to remain willingly for ever outside the national church. I cannot go back, I cannot go forward. On the tenth anniversary of my ordination I feel trapped between a Methodism which no longer satisfies but to which I am in honour bound, and an Anglicanism unwilling to accept me as I am. Between the two, I am likely to be squeezed out even further into the world.

*Monday 7 July*

Yesterday was also the 140th anniversary of the death of Sir Thomas More – the fourth of my special patron saints. More was born in 1478, and at the age of thirteen was placed in the household of Thomas Morton, Archbishop of Canterbury and Lord Chancellor. He was a merry boy, and his intellectual alertness attracted the attention of his master, who prophesied that he would prove 'a marvellous man'. When Erasmus made his first visit to England in 1497 he was introduced to Thomas More – then a young man of nineteen. This marked the beginning of a close intimacy, and they corresponded regularly with each other until separated by death.

John Richard Green describes More at this time: 'The brightness and freedom of the New Learning seemed incarnate in the young scholar, with his gay talk, his winsomeness of manner, his reckless epigrams, his passionate love of music, his omniverous reading, his paradoxical speculations, his jibes at monks, his schoolboy fervour of liberty. But events were soon to prove that beneath this sunny nature lay a stern inflexibility of conscientious resolve.'[1]

[1] J. R. Green, *A Short History of the English People*, Macmillan 1905, p. 315.

More became a member of Parliament in 1504; his famous work, *Utopia*, was published in 1516, and he was knighted in 1521. In April 1523 Wolsey recommended More's election as Speaker of the House of Commons, and six years later More succeeded him as Lord Chancellor. It was a promotion virtually without precedent: rarely had the position of Lord Chancellor been held by a layman.

As a judge, Sir Thomas More rendered his tenure of the chancellorship memorable. He encouraged suitors to resort to him at his house at Chelsea, where he would sit in his open hall, in many instances bringing the parties to a friendly reconcilement of their disputes. On the other hand, the treatment to which he subjected persons charged with heresy was severe, and his personal responsibility for the barbarous usage of many Protestants remains, in the words of Green, 'the one stain on a memory that knows no other'. He maintained a rigid distinction between the cause of reform and what seemed to him the cause of revolution. His wit seasoned his judgments, though to us the idea of merry jesting with life or liberty at stake is repugnant. One day he was examining an evangelist named Silver. 'You know,' he said with a smile, 'that silver must be tried in the fire.' 'Yes,' retorted the accused instantly, 'but not quicksilver.' More, delighted with the repartee, set the poor wretch at liberty.

Sir Thomas More resigned his office in 1532 when continuing disagreement with the king made his position impossible. On 17 April 1534 he was summoned to Lambeth to take an oath of adherence to the new Act of Succession. More declared that he could take no oath that should impugn the pope's authority or assume the justice of the king's divorce. Archbishop Cranmer bade him walk in the garden that he might reconsider his reply. 'The day was hot and More seated himself in a window from which he could look down into the crowded court. Even in the presence of death, the quick sympathy of his nature could enjoy the humour and life of the throng below. "I saw," he said afterwards, "Master Latimer very merry in the court, for he laughed and took one or twain by the neck so handsomely that if they had been women I should have weened that he waxed wanton" . . . He was called in again at last, but only repeated his refusal. It was in vain that Cranmer plied him with distinctions which perplexed even the subtle wit of the ex-chancellor; he remained unshaken and passed to the Tower.'[1] On

[1] Ibid., p. 344.

1 July 1535 he was indicted of high treason at Westminster Hall, and was found guilty. To his judges he said: 'I hope, my lords, that though you have condemned me on earth, we may all meet hereafter in heaven.'

Before nine o'clock on the morning of 6 July 1535 he was executed on Tower Hill. His composure on the scaffold was remarkable. He moved his beard carefully from the block and was heard to mutter with a touch of the old sad irony: 'Pity that should be cut – that has never committed treason.' So perished Sir Thomas More who, in the general opinion of Europe, was the foremost Englishman of his time. He was canonized in 1935.

The spell that captured Erasmus remains strong, and I derive great inspiration from the life of Sir Thomas More. His significance is summarized by Winston Churchill: 'More stood forth as the defender of all that was finest in the mediaeval outlook. He represents to history its universality, its belief in spiritual values, and its instinctive sense of other-worldliness. Henry VIII with cruel axe decapitated not only a wise and gifted counsellor, but a system which, though it had failed to live up to its ideals in practice, had for long furnished mankind with its brightest dreams.'[1]

*Tuesday 8 July*

The faces of July:

The sky was overcast, and the weather became oppressively hot this afternoon. No rain had fallen for three weeks; lawns and verges were scorched. A little rain fell this evening, and a storm broke.

Today I noticed two overpowering scents: privet and lime.

The strawberry season is at its height – to my delight!

*Wednesday 9 July*

Men and women are full of fascination, not only for what they are, but also for what they might become. I am impressed daily at the vast potential so easy to glimpse: the ideas only half-expressed; the gifts lying dormant and undeveloped; powerful and attractive personalities starving themselves to death spiritually (dominating card-schools when they could be thrilling great crowds); hopes which become more wistful as the years pass because the energy and strength of purpose to do anything about them is lacking. People are so

[1] Winston S. Churchill, *History of English-speaking Peoples*, Vol. 2, Cassell 1956, p. 52.

much more special than they give themselves credit for being; they sell themselves short, and we are all the losers. The potential is unexplored. Poems are never written that might have been written. Speeches are not made that might have been made. Paintings are not painted that might have moved and spoken to us. Songs are not composed; music is not played. It was all nearly created. And it died in the womb. The potential lies sleeping; then fades, and fades.

*Thursday 10 July*

At work today I was summoned into the office and handed a telephone. 'Someone wants to speak to you,' I was told. I listened – and received a pre-recorded Christian message! They had seen the number advertised and thought it would be just the thing for me. I was embarrassed by the content of the message – but they thought it was a huge joke to catch me in this way.

*Friday 11 July*

I have grown deeply into the life of this city: not into its establishment, civic or ecclesiastical – but amongst its people. From my cab I wave to priests and prostitutes, choir-boys and vagrants, and all sorts and conditions of men. The fact that I was born, brought up, and went to school here; the fact that I am about the streets of the city all day long; the fact that I live, preach, and work in the city centre; even the high turn-over of labour on the buses – all these have contributed to the wideness of my contacts.

*Saturday 12 July*

The gospel finds a much wider acceptance today than usually we imagine – *if the Word is made flesh*. If the gospel is presented to people in a way which suggests they must attend church (or, indeed, must *do* anything at all), they fail to see in that any good news. The gospel is a gift, not a demand. When it is made incarnate – embodied in a living person – the gospel is accepted with gladness. The good news is the offer of forgiveness, trust, reconciliation, patience, sympathy, warmth, friendship, and humility – all free and unconditional. When these are not talked about, but *given*, they are accepted far more often than they are rejected. The instances of rejection bring pain and crucifixion – and resurrection. Acceptance brings joy which is new every morning in a web of relationships precious and meaningful. This, too, is the meaning of 'presence'.

*Sunday 13 July*
More excrement in the church.

The weather is very close. After preaching tonight my clothes were soaked.

The Wedding at Cana:

Those whose religion is linked inseparably with dark clothes and hushed tones provide a strange contrast to Jesus at the party. He knew that wine and laughter, music and gaiety belonged to God's world – yes, as much as prayer and worship. The presence of Jesus at the wedding in Cana has sanctified our mirth, our music, our merrymaking. Wherever Jesus went, whenever he touched a human life, and whenever he comes into a life *now*, dullness, insipidness, and weakness become sparkling joy, and love, and strength. The water is turned to wine.

*Monday 14 July*
*Thou didst divide the sea through thy power: thou brakest the heads of the dragons in the waters.*

Many interesting people work on the buses. Tonight, for example, I spent the evening with Neill, a driver who came from another company last year. Our discussion resolved most of the outstanding human problems, after which we looked in the churches, climbed one of the towers, and finished with a couple of jars. Neill is a direct descendant, on his mother's side, of Henry James Pye (1745–1813) – the worst poet laureate in the history of English literature! Pye was appointed in 1790 by the prime minister, William Pitt. According to Sir Walter Scott, 'The poetical Pye was eminently respectable in everything but his poetry.'

*Tuesday 15 July*
During a discussion in the canteen I noted three distinct types.

Type (a) is noisy, well-known, extrovert, devil-may-care. He is a heavy drinker (when he chooses), a woman-chaser, and is domestically unsuccessful. A likeable villain. (This type is much cherished by 'evangelists').

Type (b) secretly prizes his home and family. He admires and identifies with (a) but lacks his flamboyance. Would not lightly jeopardize his domestic security; not very stimulating intellectually. A large group.

Type (c) is intelligent, interested in ideas, good at conversation; often rejects marriage as a legal institution.

Many other types can be noted; I attempt to relate to them all. Of those which impressed me today, I admire the charisma of (a), the reliability of (b), and the perception of (c).

*Wednesday 16 July*

Evensong: Bairstow in D – one of my top ten.

*I had rather be a door-keeper in the house of my God: than to dwell in the tents of ungodliness.*

Being a Christian is about being a centre of joy and love in the world, a never-varying point of total acceptance.

*Thursday 17 July*

On the way to work at six o'clock this morning I called jokingly to one of the men cleaning the windows of Marks and Spencers: 'How long must I wait before I can daub my fingers on those windows again – eight o'clock?' 'No,' he replied. 'Wait till nine – then you can piss on them if you like!' You can't say fairer than that.

*Thou spakest sometime in visions unto thy saints.*

*Friday 18 July*

*In the multitude of the sorrows that I had in my heart: thy comforts have refreshed my soul.*

The organs of the body are primarily functional, and not generally esteemed for their aesthetic qualities. However marvellous the workings of the human system, diagrams in medical books can be mildly revolting! But when those organs are bound by sinews and covered with skin, what astonishing and appealing shapes; what beauty!

*Saturday 19 July*

Brian recounted the following conversation which occurred – without a smile – at a city terminus:

Woman boarding bus: 'Do I have to take the dog upstairs?'

Brian: 'No, not unless he wants to smoke.'

Woman (reassuringly): 'Oh no – he doesn't smoke.'

She sat downstairs.

Commemoration of Bishop Herbert de Losinga, founder of the cathedral church, 1096.

*The Lord shall preserve thy going out, and thy coming in: from this time forth for evermore.*

*Sunday 20 July*
I was moved near to tears by the singing of psalm 77:
*Hath God forgotten to be gracious: and will he shut up his loving-kindness in displeasure?*

I believe that history will vindicate my 'worker-priest' ministry.

*Monday 21 July*
Received a letter from Roy Flindall, who is in Italy:

'Here in Italy . . . there is, for all the retrogressive conservatism, a genuine warmth in Catholicism which evidently springs from the people themselves. The clergy I have met are classless in a way English clergy are not. For vital religion I would opt for the Catholics of Germany, but of course they have been through the fire. For my part the evening mass in the Frauenkirche in Nuremberg was the most significant event of the week. The sense of belonging and the common purpose in worship was quite overpowering in a way I could never have suspected in England; *there* everything was fragmentary and splintered, and you always remained isolated in the crowd. (Being at that time) a lonely stranger in the city, this sense of belonging was nothing short of a life-line and answered a fundamental need. It was spiritual integration into the sacramental body, not a hearty handshake at the door or admiration for the rhetoric of the pulpit, but a deep prevailing awareness of the nature of Catholicism. This is what we lack in England. We try to manufacture community without really caring for the people or actually believing in the presence of the Spirit. Baptism is incorporation – but into what? A club for the devout. As self-preserving entities the churches lay claim to a person's continued attendance at events and the use of his gifts – and ninety-nine times out of a hundred these gifts are not those of the Spirit. Amicability and no love. The commitment demanded is to the institution in its social dimension, not to the church in its eternal aspect. The church of the kingdom is not the ultimate of faith and we have tended to fall into ecclesiastical idolatry, if only because we demand the wrong commitment from people.

When I talk of the lack of humanity in English religion, this is what I mean. The extravagance of the gospel of the kingdom requires an extravagance in Christian love, for such love is of God and not of the ethics of suburbia. Just as I believe humanism lacks true perspective in dismissing the divine (for the creativity and character of God alone give value and meaning to our acts), so I also believe English religion lacks the real human dimension. The outstretched hand is primarily there to pull the unsuspecting into the pew, in the belief that the pew is the front seat in the ark of salvation. We need to see true human values as springing from our incorporation into the life of the Trinity, and our humanity as expressive of the Spirit in our lives. The spirit of timidity regulates the work of the churches, and we are afraid to love too much because it might compromise our future. As it is, we have to turn to the unbelieving world for the exercise of charity unlimited . . . This, I think is the essence of St Francis' example – that his love for Christ, according to Chesterton, was romantic. The element of the couldn't-care-less romance of Christian love is lost under the weight of bricks and morter, committee papers, and clerical serge. If we must accept the decline of dogmatic religion, we must look for some common ground with the secular world in order to preach the gospel, and the human ground is the most obvious, immediate and urgent. I would be dishonest if I let you believe that none among the officers of the churches really have this love, but in my experience there are too few. I have found most of my good Samaritans outside the church, and a handful as exceptions within.'

*Tuesday 22 July*

I took Tony with me when I went to London today to record a television interview. London overawes me, and makes me feel ignorant and rural. I thought of this journal while walking in the Strand, and it seemed the irrelevant jottings of someone living in a rustic backwater. Yet part of me stubbornly refused to yield. The things I believe in Norwich still hold true in London: the business-man who joined in our conversation on the train was lonely and unhappy, and there were black-headed gulls on the Thames.

*Wednesday 23 July*

Two souvenirs of childhood have survived in my possession. One is a blue wooden racing-car, pockmarked with holes. I remember covering it with tin-tacks one day to make it armour-plated. The other is a book of stories and poems entitled *Wayfaring in Many Lands*,[1] with wonderful drawings I have never forgotten. The book's

[1] Stella Mead, *Wayfaring in Many Lands*, James Nisbet 1936.

survival is a miracle (for it was passed on when I grew older, and returned to me by chance), but I have only to pick it up to be back on a coconut-mat in front of the fire, wearing short trousers and chewing liquorice-root. The stories are classics: 'The Nuremburg Stove', 'Karl and the Treasure Cave', 'The Willow Pattern Plate'. My favourite was the tale of Roland and Oliver. Roland was nephew to the Emperor Charlemagne, and the story of his last stand at Roncevaux is a moving tale of treachery and love: 'Roland reached out a dying hand and touched his friend Oliver. He murmured faintly, "Oliver, thou wert the dearest of all my friends. Now thou art dead I no longer care to live." '

I can remember still the impact which that story of a legendary friendship made upon me when first I read it as a child.

*Thursday 24 July*

God is far more 'rude' than many 'godfearers' imagine. 'It is he that hath made us' (Ps. 100) and we are 'fearfully and wonderfully made' (Ps. 139).

*Friday 25 July*

I must not allow this book to degenerate into a 'Gardeners' Question-Time', but my concern is to record my thoughts and impressions, and the brightness of the flowers creates many of the most vivid impressions at this time of the year. Sweet peas and stocks are on the market stalls; phlox and hollyhocks are in full flower, with dahlias which will bloom profusely until cut down by autumn frosts, long after this diary has closed. Patches of rough ground where buildings have been demolished have undergone a transformation and are bedecked with tall clumps of golden rod, great hairy willow-herb, rose-bay willow herb, great bindweed, evening primrose.

We did a country run and at the terminus found a colony of house-martins which had nested in the outbuildings of the village pub. Tony was fascinated to see tiny faces peering out of the mud nests fixed to the underside of the rafters.

*Saturday 26 July*

This happened several years ago. Russell and Joe were 'on the carpet' and went upstairs for an interview in the superintendent's office. The door was ajar, and Joe peeped in. Seeing nobody, he slipped into the office, sat behind the desk, put his pipe in his mouth, shuffled the papers which lay in front of him, and called sharply, 'Right, Crowe! You can come in now.'

At that moment the door slowly closed – to reveal the superintendent standing behind, watching with incredulity this performance in his own office. 'Did you want anything, Ferris?' he barked. Joe leapt to his feet as though he'd been stung. 'No sir – sorry sir – sorry sir,' was the only explanation he could manage. He backed out of the room as the superintendent advanced threateningly.

'You're a comedian, Ferris.'

Words failed completely. Only nods of agreement would come. Nod-nod-nod.

'You're wasted here.'

Nod-nod-nod.

'You should be on the stage.'

Nod-nod-nod.

But he's still here!

*Sunday 27 July*

Worked an early shift. Tonight I enjoyed Terence Rattigan's *The Deep Blue Sea* on television.

*Monday 28 July*

Molly says that since I became a busman, there is not a clergyman for whom I have a good word to say. I think that is a little harsh; but perhaps I am beginning to think and feel like someone who is a non-churchman. This I will admit – that many clergymen strike me as being not only upper-middle class in their demeanour, but incredibly immature in their behaviour. Often they embarrass me with a kind of childishness which would not go down well in our canteen. We could do with more clergy who combined sternness with tenderness, dignity with warmth, strictness with compassion, manliness with receptivity.

*Tuesday 29 July*

With the temperature soaring into the eighties, the buses have become almost unbearable.

Over a pint, Stephen described the week he spent walking in the Lake District. His enthusiasm was such that he made it sound like a profound religious experience – which, in fact, I think it was.

*Wednesday 30 July* 

This friend has suffered with schizophrenia; formerly he taught history, but now he works with us. He described the effects of his drugs and the cruel choice they inflict: 'I can either take the drugs and lead a balanced life but forfeit my gifts and intellectual abilities, or I can refuse the drugs and regain my gifts and insight but lose the ability to lead a normal routine.' I found our conversation exceptionally valuable.

As I made my way home I saw a swallow-tailed moth flitting among the heavily-scented hemp agrimony; there were five swans on the dark river.

*Thursday 31 July*

Although I use the word 'love' constantly, I cannot define it. In all their different contexts, sacred or profane, the meanings of the word seem ultimately to be linked. *The Symposium* is inspiring; *Agape and Eros* is powerful; but I can only ponder, and marvel.

Love is warmth, attraction, desire, affinity; love is compassion, tenderness, self-sacrifice, service; love is friendship; love is copulation; love is worship; love is nameless. Any tentative reaching-out from the inner citadel of our own self-consciousness towards another self is love.

It's bloody hot in this bus.

It seems clear that *emotionally* human nature is fundamentally bisexual (which makes nonsense of the antagonism between heterosexuals and homosexuals). A layer of bisexuality undoubtedly exists in a great number of people. Its forms of expression depend on the depth of the layer, but it is the fountain of all friendship, comradeship, companionship, and warmth. We know it – and if we were not so irrationally terrified of anything that might be construed as homosexuality, we would admit it to ourselves. The abuse of society and the outraged morality of the church are irrelevant if a fact happens to be true – and no sympathetic study of human nature can fail to note the close ties of acceptance, respect, and affection which decline to conform to the sexual boundaries. Yet we are not prepared to recognize the reality. She must not love her; he must not feel affection towards him . . . What pathetic rubbish! To experience any kind of 'togetherness', any pleasure in another's company, is pure and good and refreshing and liberating; a miracle; a mystery.

Alas, the very vehemence with which ideas of this kind are repudiated is in itself evidence of our spiritual-sexual uncertainty. How sad that the natural, intuitive sexual flow has to be checked in this unnecessary way; that the magic of romance has to be denied; that the mystery, the joy, and the enrichment of any loving relationship should be unacknowledged; that it should be a sin to love too much, or to feel warmth for the wrong sort of people. Is there so much love and friendship in the world that we can afford to throw some away? Is there so much gladness and mutual recognition that we need carefully to discriminate? We are people first, and possessors of genitalia second; the differences between the sexes enhance life, but have relatively little to do with the sheer enjoyment of a person as a human being. Children know this intuitively: but we soon correct them, and instil our fears and hatreds.

It is, of course, the physical implications which terrify us. 'We all like to have good mates – but we don't want to go to bed with them!' There it is again – that deadly conflict between mind and body. These implications are utterly beside the point. Nobody is advocating specific physical practices, or any practices at all. But how wonderful if we dared admit our warmth and our closeness, without shame; and dared to give it a name.

*Friday 1 August*

Neville, one of my former conductors (now a student at university), called this afternoon.

My summer holiday started today. I think this *is* significant: I'm genuinely a little sad when my holiday begins to think I won't see everyone again for a fortnight! That is more the reaction of the pastor than the busman.

*Saturday 2 August*

Ten years ago an old, wizened, witch-like woman I visited in a remote Fenland hamlet said to me: 'How long have you been a minister? You speak the language of the common labourer.' I can't remember her name, and her ancient cottage has probably been demolished; but often I recall her words. She was as a messenger of God to me, and I vowed that any gift she divined should be used to his glory.

*Sunday 3 August*

I read in the *Methodist Recorder* part of the Revd A. Raymond George's presidential address to the Methodist Conference: '. . . Moreover, in the language of theology, God is not only immanent, but transcendent. We are not pantheists; a God sharply defined is better than a God so thinly spread that he is nowhere in particular. Incarnational religion does not mean that God, or Christ, is incarnate everywhere, but that God is uniquely incarnate in Jesus Christ; yet there is an incarnational principle, a scandal of particularity, which runs through church and sacraments, and it summons us not only to that diffuse prayer and worship which is the Christian life in general, but to the concentrated expression of it in particular times of prayer and worship.

Worship is not a means to a good life, the support of Christian living. It is a foretaste of heaven, where there is no question of striving towards a goal, or producing a good result, or even of evangelism or service, but all is pure joy. It is, as has been said, an eschatological game, or from the point of view of productivity, a glorious waste of time. "To what purpose is this waste?" said some who were present when a woman anointed Jesus. The only reply is that there can be no further end beyond glorifying God.'

*Monday 4 August*

I sat on the beach at Cromer and read Thomas Mann's *Death in Venice*: 'How dare you smile like that! No one is allowed to smile like that!'

*Tuesday 5 August*

Today brought back many memories. It was spent by a stream, helping the children to catch bullheads, loach, and dace. The day was very hot. I admired some clumps of tansy. Two of our garden tiger moths emerged from their chrysalides this evening.

*Wednesday 6 August*

The feast of the Transfiguration of Christ.

There are many ways of interpreting experience – and people lie when they pretend to be no-nonsense, scientific materialists all the time. We treat no person as fifty-pence-worth of miscellaneous chemicals – much less someone we love. We apply a different method of evaluation. The body is not just clay. On that we all agree. But by that very reckoning, the sun becomes more than just gas, and the moon more than a cold lump of lifeless rock; a church becomes more than just an old building, a promise more than mere words. All is transfigured.

*Thursday 7 August*

I attended holy communion on the feast of the Name of Jesus.

The harvest is in full swing. With the temperature soaring into the nineties we visited the wildlife park at Great Witchingham. I enjoyed particularly seeing the animals and birds which are on the British lists but which most of us seldom have an opportunity to watch: ravens, polecats, a snowy owl, short-eared owls, otters, badgers, white storks, a fox, pine martens, little owls, oyster-catchers, curlews, grey seals, common seals, whooper swans, a nut-hatch, and a golden eagle.

*Friday 8 August*

Back to the beach today.

Is Christianity concerned with wild, unconfined love or not? Or is it concerned with a theological abstract?

*Saturday 9 August*

I don't remember it being as hot as this since I was a small boy. After lying awake for an hour, I rose at a quarter past five, made a pot of tea, and went for a stroll along Quayside. Two boys were pulling out some good bream, and fish were surfacing noisily in all directions. The sun was fiery red low in the east, and a family of wrens were chattering noisily. Most commotion, however, came from the moorhens. A pair of adult birds were busy strengthening their nest, on which were perched fluffy black chicks. This task is never-ending on a flowing river, and the parents were assisted by a survivor from the first brood, who brought sticks as faithfully as the others. I watched this activity with interest, but when the five swans sailed slowly past in line astern their haughty indifference showed plainly that they had seen it all before.

Evensong: Stanford in B flat.

*For this God is our God for ever and ever: he shall be our guide unto death.*

*Sunday 10 August*
Two contrasting impressions: the sheer, frightening power of passion; mountain ash berries – one of the earliest hints of autumn.

*Monday 11 August*
Two beautiful things: a wall butterfly on the mint flowers in the garden; a small colony of kittiwakes, gliding from their nests on the cliffs.

*Tuesday 12 August*
I wonder how Tony is managing without me! I spared a thought for him as I swam and sunbathed. I swim like a heavily-laden amphibious army-vehicle.

This evening I visited South Creake parish church for the monthly office of the Guild of the Servants of the Sanctuary. There is a quality about mediaeval architecture which is inspiring and ennobling before ever a word is uttered: and this church is a gem. It was a warm, still summer evening, quiet and perfect. Darkness fell during the service, and the incense and flickering candles said more about the eternal God than most of our with-it attempts to make him 'relevant'. Afterwards there was good beer and good comapny; the day was a splendid contribution to a holiday, by any reckoning.

*Wednesday 13 August*
I lazed on the beach and in the sea, with the best tan I've ever had. Tonight I felt I'd had too much sun, but a couple of pints pulled me round. I told the story of the driver who closed the electrically-operated doors on his bus, and cut the tops off a bunch of daffodils being held by a woman on the platform! She gazed at her stalks with a look of unbelief.

*Thursday 14 August*
We went for a ride up the river, through the heart of the city, in a steam-powered launch seventy years old. One buddleia overhanging the water was smothered with peacock butterflies.

I was shown the pre-1662 collect for Trinity XVIII; it is worth using: 'Lord, we beseech thee, grant thy people grace to escape the infections of the devil, and with pure heart and mind to follow thee, the only God: through Jesus Christ our Lord. Amen.'

*Friday 15 August*

The sea was choppy today, but still I had a swim. (Actually, Trevor went in first; with secret reluctance – it was cold – I had to follow to save face.)

Often, I am told by churchmen: 'We respect you for doing what you feel you ought to do, but we don't understand what you hope to prove.' Non-churchmen seem to understand much more easily.

*Saturday 16 August*

Tonight, in the pub, I realized again that many people will never go to church. In the words of George Eliot: 'We must learn to accommodate ourselves to the discovery that some of those cunningly-fashioned instruments called human souls have only a very limited range of music, and will not vibrate in the least under a touch that fills others with tremulous rapture or quivering agony.' I do not believe these are bound unerringly for hell. They are among the 'other sheep I have, which are not of this fold', and they are included in my ministry – indeed, it is becoming increasingly directed towards them. I began by requesting pastoral charge of a congregation and permission to work (and minister) in the world. Without forming societies or seeing conversions – which the 'religious' mind could have grasped and understood – the web of relationships I have established in the world has started to demand more of *myself* (my time, my physical presence); this leaves less time for the preparation and conduct of services for tiny pockets of the faithful. Worship has not become secondary, or less important – and it would be misery for me not to preach. It is a question of stewardship and priorities.

*Sunday 17 August*

This was the last day of my holiday. I used the opportunity to visit a church where the worship differs from that to which normally I am accustomed. The service was a procession and solemn mass of the Assumption of the Blessed Virgin Mary. I learnt two new tunes: St Alban ('Ave Maria! blessed Maid!'), and Farley Castle ('Her Virgin eyes saw God incarnate born').

George Eliot refers to Methodism: '. . . an amphitheatre of green hills, or the deep shade of broad-leaved sycamores, where a crowd of rough men and weary-hearted women drank in a faith which was a rudimentary culture, which linked their thoughts with the past, lifted their imagination above the sordid details of their own narrow lives, and suffused their souls with the sense of a pitying, loving, infinite Presence . . .' Methodists developed into 'that modern type which reads quarterly reviews and attends in chapels with pillared porticoes'; she describes 'sleek grocers, sponging preachers, and hypocritical jargon' – and surely would have enjoyed *Anna of the Five Towns*.

The Methodism of the eighteenth century, evoked so skilfully in that first description, is the Methodism dear to me: the Methodism of Wesley's hymns and powerful preaching. But clear traces of both those pen-pictures could be identified in the Methodism I joined twenty years ago. It is so no longer. The distinctive Methodist ethos is shrivelling; the decay of the last two decades is astonishing. Old members have died, and where they have been followed it has been by a new type of church-member, often with little feeling for the tradition of the denomination. There has been a loss of identity – and it has gone for ever. After two hundred years, my denomination is searching for its soul – but the old fires will be rekindled only when Methodism is set in a larger, Catholic context.

*Monday 18 August*

Back to work! First impressions after a holiday are of the noise and vibrations in the cab, but soon these wear off. Tony gave me all the news for the past fortnight: who had the sack, who had the big accident, the rotten shifts I missed, the drivers he had in my place, Norwich City's terrible start to the season . . . (We scarcely touch on religion. He doesn't believe in it. I would be a fool to risk losing a good conductor for the sake of a little cheap 'evangelism'.)

*Tuesday 19 August*

If I had been willing to cheat, I would have made this the last entry in the book. It would have neatly rounded off my diary, and throughout the evening I kept thinking: 'This is where I came in!' Charles – to whose spectacular bus-driving career I have referred – has gone to live in a windmill on the Norfolk Broads, and Stephen and I went to visit him this afternoon. It was last 2 September over again!

After examining the mill and giving our unqualified approval, we went for a row on the river, treating horrified anglers and mystified holidaymakers in their cruisers to scenes reminiscent of Jerome K. Jerome. Charles prepared an excellent supper, and while it was cooking he and I sang Gilbert and Sullivan, fortissimo. During this episode Steve withdrew discreetly to a safe distance, preferring communion with nature to fellowship with a mutilated captain of the *Pinafore*. Bats flitted overhead, the ground was littered with tiny frogs, a wren kept darting about near the door – while the marsh was a solid blaze of purple loosestrife.

After supper, we smoked and talked; again our conversation ranged over a wide selection of topics – from Gresley 'Pacifics' to why it is that often we behave in a manner we know to be less than the best of which we are capable. We recalled our evening together last autumn, (and the big barmaid), and they laughed at the memory of my apostasy. Pierced to the quick, I countered by reminding Steve of how he was sick outside the pub, afterwards. Stricken with galloping amnesia (even as I spoke), he attempted to deny this – but I was not to be gainsaid. 'Oh yes you were,' I roared accusingly (sending up a small flock of mallard), 'because I was on an early shift next morning, and on the way to work I saw the pigeons eating it.' The defence collapsed.

I tried to persuade big, bearded Charles to sing 'I'm called Little Buttercup' one more time, but was outvoted by Stephen who threatened to bash my face in. It was a lively evening, and we missed the last bus from the nearest village. (Happily, we didn't *just* miss it: we were lying back in our chairs, laughing loudly, when suddenly it occurred to someone that the bus had long since gone.) We left the mill reluctantly, and walked back slowly along a narrow footpath between tall trees which brought us to the road; we each had a pint at The Black Horse.

The moon had fought free of the clouds, and it was not easy to turn again towards the city. We bid farewell to Charles, and started the long walk to the nearest bus route. Steve assured me, however, that he would be able to thumb a lift for us. The first set of headlights appeared, with the deep rumble of a lorry engine. 'Leave it to me,' I was commanded, in a voice that oozed confidence. I did as I was told, and stood meekly on the verge – as the lorry sped past. 'Thank goodness that didn't stop!' – I gave a heart-felt gasp. 'Why?' snapped my irritated companion. 'It was the night-soil cart,' I replied mildly. 'Shit!' he shouted up the road. (More mallard went up.)

We marched on in the moonlight, whistling excruciating military airs to keep in step. Steve sang 'Colonel Bogey' – this, obviously, was what he'd been saving himself for – and I struck up 'From the sunny Spanish shore' (all four parts), but was outvoted once more. Stephen announced that he would need to make a brief stop; two seconds later a police car pulled out of a gateway (as is their wont) and caught him full beam. With many respectful waves and cries of 'Good evening, officer', finally we found a bus; our colleague shot a quizzical glance, but refrained – somewhat pointedly, one felt – from asking what we were doing in such a place at such an hour. It had been a wonderful visit. I'm too tired, tonight, to raise phoney philosophical questions about it, to be poetic about the beauty and peace of the creation, or to apologize for my crudeness. I simply enjoyed it all – every second.

*Wednesday 20 August*

This month I have read *Maurice* by E. M. Forster; *Adolf Hitler – My Part in His Downfall* by Spike Milligan (which made me re-read *Puckoon*); and – as the experts will have discerned already – have made a start on George Eliot's *Adam Bede*.

I worked a split-shift today, into which I inserted some study and typing. Afterwards, Tony and I had a quick jar, collected Trevor, and watched an entertaining football match against Leeds United which ended in a 1–1 draw. It was a straightforward yet ridiculously happy day. I enjoy life so much. All right – I am lucky, many times over; for some life is hard. But I could wish there was more enjoyment in the world – more gratitude, more awareness, more gladness, more acceptance, more light-heartedness, more friendship, more reverence, more fun. I wish everyone tonight could be as happy as I am. I hope that doesn't sound pious or trite. I have no savings in the bank but today, once again, I was given – a day!

*Thursday 21 August*

I had my annual argument as to whether or not lupins have a scent. Some say not, but they have, of course – a spicy, elusive, evocative scent which I find exciting: it is a hint, a longing, a memory. (I can recall sniffing these flowers as a small child, before I needed to bend down to reach them.) Scent is the Cinderella of the human senses. Unlike many animals, we have not developed this capacity to any degree, and there must be a vast range of stimulating scents which escape our detection. Nonetheless, the garden offers a surprising variety of plants which – in flower and foliage – provide a wide selection of distinct scents. Wallflowers are completely different from roses (which themselves vary enormously), and marigold leaves are nothing like those of the nasturtium. In winter months, blue sweet violets and snowdrops are scented with a fragrance which is unusually affecting. Alison Uttley writes in *A Year in the Country*: 'When I see the tight little bunches of closed buds in the shops and I smell that strangely moving scent of snowdrops, half bitter, half earthy, my heart misses a beat. They appear on the greengrocer's shelf, so small, so quiet, with a few ivy leaves round them, so modest among the freesias and the hyacinths, but they are quickly snapped up and the rich flowers are left.'[1]

In springtime the scent of gathered primroses and cowslips has the powerful ability to whisk you away for a split second from wherever you may be and to set you down in warm sunshine on a grassy bank, with nesting birds calling loudly and the hedgerows bedecked in fresh green. None of the other senses can create this kind of impression and experience so instantly and overwhelmingly. As spring merges into early summer the big red peonies burst open with that magical scent I inhale deeply, over and over again. It is sweet, yet dark and mysterious and sensual; a fulfilment. (Pink and white peonies, a few weeks later, have an entirely different scent.) Honeysuckle, lilies, sweet peas – the summer list is endless; carnations, stocks, geraniums – each may be easily recognized.

The frosts and mists of autumn bring the scent of dying leaves and, for me, the epitome of autumn: the scent of chrysanthemums. Then it is winter again. Alison Uttley describes her house at Christmas time: 'The scent of the woods is strong, the fragrance of moss and leaves, of fir boughs and crushed rosemary comes from the decorations as one enters the room. It is companionable and good, the odour of the earth which we so often forget.'[2]

*Friday 22 August*

'Everything exists for itself, yet everything is part of something else' – Wilhelm Reich.

Brian is so dead-pan I almost feel sorry for his victims. A woman

[1] Alison Uttley, *A Year in the Country*, Faber & Faber 1957, pp. 47f.

[2] Ibid., p. 25.

approached him in the bus station yard and said: 'Please can you tell me when the Ipswich bus goes?'

'I'm dreadfully sorry,' he replied confidentially, 'but we're not allowed to divulge secret information. You must ask an inspector.'

'Oh yes, of course – I'm sorry,' she whispered back – and hurried to find an inspector.

*Saturday 23 August*

My scholarly old friend told me of a prayer-desk he used to have in his church. It came from the chapel of the nearby American Air Force base, and was given to him at the end of the war. (It is now in an American War Museum.) The desk had been made on the camp out of wooden bomb-crates, and under the varnish could be read the words FULLY FUSED. He said, 'I saw them whenever I knelt to pray, and thought: "This is a word for me; Lord, let my prayers be fully fused." '

*Sunday 24 August*

Sermon: 'I Believe in God.'

Every man needs some kind of faith or belief by which to live, and every man formulates his personal convictions out of his own experience of life. My belief in God arises out of my awareness and my experience of the natural order of which I form a part. I am aware of my own existence. I am alive – a rational being with a self-consciousness and a self-awareness which has unfolded and developed since my birth. I *am* – a lonely, inner, mysterious reality – perched upon a planet, whirling through space. It is these basic facts of my existence which fill me with awe, and prompt long periods of reflection. For I cannot help wondering if the countless forms of life and existence which comprise the creation are controlled by blind, nameless, abstract forces, or by a supreme reason. And I discover that man – since first he became capable of such thought – has always pondered these matters. When confronted by phenomena which he could not understand, or which he feared, primitive man responded by offering worship. And I have never felt that our incomparably more complex scientific understanding has destroyed or lessened the central mystery. In our astonishing age – where new discoveries and achievements are matched only by the speed with which we take them completely for granted – I am impressed that space-journeys can be timed to the split-second with an utter depen-

dence upon the reliability of the cosmos. Perhaps I am a person of excessive simplicity, but I can still feel – after two and a half thousand years – total sympathy with the psalmist when he gazes up at the night sky and murmurs: 

> I will consider thy heavens, even the works of thy fingers:
> the moon and the stars, which thou hast ordained.
> What is man, that thou art mindful of him? (Ps. 8)

I am still thrilled – almost violently stirred – when the setting sun shines through the dust of the earth's atmosphere: and we see a magnificent sunset. I hear incommunicable messages when a series of sounds are arranged in order and in harmony and in contrast: a symphony! I peer through a microscope at normally invisible existences, and feel a sense of reverence. I listen to a science-master speaking about the mystery of matter – protons, neutrons, electrons – and I am convinced that the universe has some secret, hidden, life, and that man is only a part of something infinitely greater. This is the beginning of my belief in God: a sense of awe, wonder, mystery, 'otherness', and reverence. I do not extol ignorance and superstition, and disparage disciplined learning and scientific investigation. On the contrary, I find that greater knowledge tends to enhance my ability and my inclination to marvel. I cannot think of God as a being standing outside the creation, looking in, but as the motivating and sustaining force within creation – what Wordsworth in the 'Lines written above Tintern Abbey' called

> A motion and a spirit, that impels
> All thinking things, all objects of all thought,
> And rolls through all things.

For me, God is (a) the ultimate source of energy and matter, (b) the creative power that designs and holds matter together in millions of different shapes and forms, and (c) the source of all life. Thus, by definition, the vital question for me is not 'Does God exist?', but 'Is God personal?' Is the power that holds stars in their courses abstract, or is it personality capable of relationship? It – or he/she?

It is at this point that the church comes into my thinking. For just as I find myself set in a fascinating world of natural splendour, which causes me to wonder about its origin and maintenance, so too I find in existence in human society – among many other groups and religions – a peculiar organization called 'the church'. It is an enigma in itself. It speaks of reconciliation, yet is itself woefully divided. It offers 'salvation' from the influences that blight human life, yet its members are not particularly noted, en masse, for their poise and integrity. It claims to be a movement of world-revolution, yet finds it painfully difficult to adjust and move from one age to another. But the detailed history of this strange movement can be plainly traced, and it dates back nearly two thousand years. It was established by Jesus of Nazareth, and sprang from the ancient Jewish religious tradition. That Jesus existed historically I would have thought we need have little doubt; what we decide about his significance is another matter. But grasp the enormity of the church's belief! The fundamental message of the church is that in this man, the creator spirit – the eternal Source of energy and form and life – revealed himself to men in a necessarily restricted yet essentially complete fashion. The holy scriptures of the church declare that 'In the beginning was the Word (i.e. Christ), and the Word was with God, and the Word was God . . . All things were made by him . . . And the Word was made flesh, and dwelt among us . . . And we beheld his glory' (John 1.1–14); 'He is the image of the invisible God . . . By him were all things created, visible and invisible . . . All things were created by him, and for him . . . And by him all things consist (Col. 1.15f.); 'In him we live, and move, and have our being' (Acts 17.28).

This is the power which was concentrated, and translated into the comprehensible, everyday terms of human existence, in the life of Jesus of Nazareth (says the church). And it is when I look at Jesus of Nazareth that my belief in God begins to come alive. Despite all I have said about the wonders of the created order, I am not a nature-worshipper. The creation thrills and frightens me, with its beauty and its immensity. But when I listen to this man talking about God and man, his words seem to strike a chord already there, deep within. For me, many of his sayings possess what I can only describe as a self-evident authority. When he speaks of the attitudes I should display, and the kind of person I ought to be, I find – to my amazement – that I feel instinctively his words are true – deeply, vitally true. He said: 'I am the Way, the Truth, and the Life', and everything within me shouts 'Yes'. My ultimate, burning question had become 'Is God personal?' I thought it likely – indeed, almost logically necessary – for we ourselves are persons, and the creature surely cannot be more advanced than its creator, nor separate from its sustainer. But this Jesus answered my question with a thrilling simplicity: he taught that we should address the eternal Spirit – who is not, in fact, only personality, but complex relationship soaring beyond our understanding – as father! Not abstract, but a person. Not indifferent, still less malevolent; but love. And I believe in God because I believe in Jesus of Nazareth. I believe he lived; I believe in his teaching that the way of love – even when it leads to crucifixion – is the only way that leads to joy and to fulfilment; I believe that he was a unique manifestation in human form of ultimate reality.

Last – but by no means least – I believe in God because I believe I have experienced his love. My personal convictions belong to me alone, and I do not expect them to convince anybody else about anything. Others may well conclude that my experience is worthless – all delusion, wishful-thinking, and emotion. But it is *my* experience, and it is not worthless to me. And my deepest conviction is that because Jesus was the man from God, he is a present power to be reckoned with in the world, and not merely a historical character. It is my conviction that through devotion and discipleship he renews my spirit and my outlook, and brings me into a new and meaningful harmony with the creation: with both the world itself and with the people in it. (How feeble words become!) Through my acceptance of the way of love as my ideal, I believe God has altered the direction of my life and the basic nature of my character. I believe that human life gives the deepest gladness when it is lived in harmony with the will and spirit of Jesus. I believe that God loves all his creation. These things have not been demonstrated to me scientifically. (Perhaps love and existence can never be proved, but only experienced.) Neither have I captured God. I have not been able to neatly label him and tailor him to my own requirements. He eludes me, and I doubt. Yet of all these things I have become convinced. I have noticed my attitudes change. And I have discovered where peace, and patience, and forgiveness, and strength, and other secret inner resources are to be found.

I believe in God, therefore, through the 'evidence' of the creation, the church, and what I believe to be my personal experience. My beliefs are not constant. I am a weak and selfish person, and need to be converted new every morning. There are many doctrines of which I am uncertain; many things I ought to believe but cannot; a vast catalogue of items I cannot begin to understand, and which constantly threaten to overwhelm the little faith I have. But I believe, again, that the planets are held in place by almighty love. I believe – in the words of that great preacher Dr W. E. Sangster – 'that God is on the throne of the universe, and God is Love. I will hold to that. For the rest, I can wait.'

(The outline of this sermon was first produced for one of my former conductors; I include it here as a summary of many of the things I have tried to say.)

*Monday 25 August*

A Bank Holiday, but Tony and I were detailed to work.

Douglas Thompson said a few years ago (in an article in the 1966 report of the Methodist Missionary Society): 'Christians pray for "showers of blessing" and plaintively sing "Let some drops now fall on me . . ." But out in the schools, and the streets, and among men and women there is already "the sound of abundance of rain". Will the church get out and get wet? So often when the downpour is at its height we hear it on our church roof and complain that "that secularism" is making so much noise we can't hear the prayers.'

I'm soaked; and it's gloriously invigorating.

*Tuesday 26 August*

A very early shift this morning. It came as a shock to find it was still almost dark when I had to get up. The summer is passing. As I walked to work mist was rising off the river, and the lightly-veiled cathedral spire looked ghostly and ethereal, like a tower of Camelot.

This afternoon I visited a former busman in prison, and later completed a manuscript upon which I've spent many hours: a careful editing of Wesley's eucharistic hymns, the neglect of which I consider a scandal. A church which is careless of such treasure *deserves* chastisement.

*Wednesday 27 August*

As usual, a whole series of thoughts in the cab . . . the field where I saw gulls following the plough last October, and later noted the fresh green winter barley coming through, is now a field of stubble once again. A year has all but turned, and the gardens are bright with asters . . . a lot of scruffy parsons about, combining the clerical-collar with an assortment of casual-wear . . . pain is a terrible mystery, much to be avoided yet possessing power not only to destroy but also to refine character. I am apprehensive, because I fear there is much that cannot be understood without pain . . . everyone likes to tell others what they ought to do; I hate being told . . . the no pre-marital sex battle has been lost by the church, ages ago, and we might as well accept the fact; youngsters have shaken off time-honoured fears and taboos, and there is nothing we can do about it. It may be cause for regret, but we make ourselves look silly if we pretend they are only holding hands . . . we haven't found any privet hawk moth caterpillars yet; we like to keep some pupae during the winter, and enjoy the newly-emerged moths in July. We found two pale prominent caterpillars, with the double black and yellow line along each side, and these have turned into pupae. But we badly want some privet hawks.

A former busman called tonight to drag me out for a pint (I'm glad to say).

*Thursday 28 August*

A foggy morning which set hundreds of spiders' webs glistening. The meadow at Costessey was full of thistledown. Roy, on holiday, sent me a postcard of preserved LNER A4 No. 4498 'Sir Nigel Gresley'.

*Sehon king of the Amorites: for his mercy endureth for ever; And Og the king of Basan: for his mercy endureth for ever.*

*Friday 29 August*

Tony and I were delighted this morning to see a lorry from Lancashire which belonged to B. Swindell.

They don't seem to write tunes like those which blared through the wireless when I was a small boy and everyone listened to 'Music While You Work'. Often, as today, I find myself humming in the cab: 'Moonlight Madonna'; 'Shine through my Dreams'; 'Mary'; and other *real* songs.

*Saturday 30 August*

In an old *Methodist Recorder* I rediscovered an article by Frederick C. Gill on the importance of the Christian calendar:

'How much we lose by neglecting the Christian year! To earlier generations the passage of time, marked by the great festivals, carried a colour and significance hardly known in a secular age and brought a pattern of meaning into everyday life. The calendar came alive and the festivals were exhilarating. The counting of time without reference to traditional values is prosaic and impoverishing, for the saints' days and feasts highlight creative periods of the past, the recollection of which adds an enrichment to life which no civil holidays can replace . . . they have a strong human as well as devotional value and link us to a thousand generations.

The ancient fairs of Britain – those mammoth jollifications which crowded the market places and sprawled across the commons – followed the Christian calendar, some like that of St Bartholomew bearing the names of saints. This was in an age when there was a lesser gulf between the maypole and the church, and when dancing was natural both in the churchyard and on the green. It was a period when life was structured by a common faith, and it was a faith rooted in the work and revelry of men.

The comic element in the miracle plays, with their combination of liturgy and farce, shows how the church borrowed, and transformed to its own use, not only pagan rites but popular forms of amusement . . . 'Do not,' said Gregory the Great to his missionaries, 'pull down the pagan temples or abolish the ancient rites, but use them for God's greater glory.' As for the ancient feasts and sacrifices: 'Let these become a social meal in honour of him whom they now worship.' Thus arose, for example, the Church Ale, which was the transformation of a pagan libation. And because life then was mainly agricultural these customs and festivals matched the cycle of the seasons, like Plough Monday, Rogation Days, May Day, and Lammas tide.

It was a time too when men rejoiced to be alive and their festivals in consequence were exuberant and often ran to excess, but even if ill-regulated, they reflected a strong sense of life and a religious faith linked to a lusty vitality. Have we become too civilized to appreciate this instinctive feeling and this rough but natural zest, for though today we prolong life, we seem hardly to be in love with it, in our preoccupation with war, neurosis, drugs, violence and talk of the meaninglessness of existence and of the death of God.

Observance of the Christian year holds a Christian to his faith and a nation to its background. Christians, above all, should observe what the calendar so plainly offers . . . For here in logical sequence is the gospel theme. All is dramatized, from Advent to Easter and on to Pentecost and the feast of All Saints, each with its recurring reminder of divine redeption and human destiny . . .

Truth lies not in the clouds but in the everyday life of men, of which the calendar is a daily reminder, and no religion which remains remote from human activity can satisfy the heart. Herein lies the genius of the Christian year, which marks not only the passing of time but also the march of the Spirit. It depicts in human terms the timeless pilgrimage of Christ, from the cradle to the grave and on to his glory. It reflects, day by day, life's inner meaning, and also that eternal dimension in which no calendar finds a place. And if, like our forbears, we give secular meaning to religious observances and add revelry and mirth to our holy occasions, we are in good company. For all their riotous abandon, holidays were holy days. All was related and harmonious, not broken and disjointed as today. All was good: the soil, the seasons, food, drink and every wholesome thing. And life itself was good, not to be rejected, but to be used and enjoyed to the full in every golden moment. The Christian drama was re-enacted each year – in vivid mime and feast and solemn celebration, adding grace and poetry, and carrying down the years a living sense of God and of the relevance of the Christian faith.'

*Sunday 31 August*

'Ye are the salt of the earth,' said our Lord. Our task is to season, to nourish, to leaven. How the world needs this seasoning! But the salt is locked away. It's in the church safe, guarded by ministers whose chief concern is to keep the church machine ticking over. We don't want to dirty it, or contaminate it; therefore we shall lose it. The salt will decompose and waste and lose its savour unless we are prepared to use it. It is decomposing already. We are losing the power of the Holy Spirit and the compulsion to mission, and time and again we offer stones instead of bread. Salt that has lost its savour is a soggy, useless mess. No wonder we feel no great urgency to get into the pubs and among the people; perhaps it's because we've nothing to give.

We say that the world needs the church and its gospel. I believe it is equally true that the church needs the world. If we are content that our religion be a hobby and the church a club, then we shall decay in an isolated byway while the life of the world rushes past untouched and unredeemed. But the moment we venture deliberately into the world, eager to provide a Christian presence and willing for the gospel to be made flesh in us, our religion springs instantly to life because we are thrown back upon the Holy Spirit. Away from church premises and practices and regulations, we tread new ground. The doctrines at the centre of our faith – the cross and the atonement, the kingdom, the new birth, the Holy Spirit, the means of grace – all are thrown into clear focus and assume new vitality. In the context of the world, faced by the forces of evil and the needs of men and women, our religion comes into its own. None of this should surprise us, for is not ours the religion of the God who left the skies because he cared for the world, who left the quietness of temple and countryside to be with the masses, who flouted the proprieties of the day by going to be the guest of a man that was a sinner? 'This man receiveth sinners, and eateth with them!' Amen and Amen!

Holiness is about the quality of our relationships in the world; it has little to do with trying to hide from the world and its evil influences. Are we more 'holy' than our Lord? He mixed, easily and naturally, with all sorts and conditions of men. But we share the embarrassment and the genuine perplexity of the pharisees, and are uncomfortable in the presence of his friends. 'Why, Lord, why?' we ask. And the answer is simple and eternal: 'I came not to call the righteous, but sinners to repentance.'

*Monday 1 September*

So that's it! Day by day the seasons have come and gone, bearing new delights and carrying them away. A year has passed, and the diary ends – but a fresh working-week has begun, and here's a new day! Communicants were entering the church of St Giles for early mass on their patronal festival . . . the boys on the building site – scorched by the heat of this exceptional summer – whistle loudly whenever a pretty girl walks by . . . bright stones which glistened on the sea-shore and were brought home by the children during the holiday now lie dull and uninteresting in the garden, no longer beautiful away from the touch of the sea . . . I saw a garden full of autumn crocuses . . . Tony again collected record takings, and blamed me for picking up too many people! . . . God is good.

I have kept the last word for Adelaide Anne Procter (1825–1864):

I thank Thee, too, that all our joy
   Is touched with pain;
That shadows fall on brightest hours;
   That thorns remain;
So that earth's bliss may be our guide,
   And not our chain.

I thank Thee, Lord, that here our souls,
   Though amply blest,
Can never find, although they seek,
   A perfect rest,
Nor ever shall, until they lean
   On Jesu's breast.

## *ACKNOWLEDGMENTS*

The publishers are grateful to the following for permission to reproduce photographs:

'Eastern Daily Press', Norwich, page 146; Eric Hosking and Royal Society for the Protection of Birds, 190; Jarrold & Sons Ltd, 117; London Weekend Television, 168; The Rt Revd Eric Treacy, 48.

The quotations on pages 78f. from *Lady Chatterley's Lover* (1928; full edition published 1960), the essay *A Propos of Lady Chatterley's Lover* (1930; now included as a preface to the present edition of the novel) and *Women in Love* (1930) are included by kind permission of the publishers, William Heinemann Ltd, Laurence Pollinger Ltd and the Estate of the late Mrs Frieda Lawrence.